The Productivity Method

How To Stop Procrastination and Get More Done

Chris Allen

Copyright © Allen Publishing

All rights reserved.
No part of this publication may be reproduced, distributed, or transmitted in any form or by any means, including photocopying, recording, or other electronic or mechanical methods, without the prior written permission of the publisher, except in the case of brief quotations embodied in critical reviews and certain other non-commercial uses permitted by copyright law.

Table of Contents

It's Time To Solve The Procrastination Puzzle

Real Life Case Study: Gayle

Real Life Case Study: Simon

Real Life Case Study: Joseph

Real Life Case Study: Serena

Chapter One – Effective Time Management

Where You Need To Be

Chapter Two – The Productivity Factors

Real Life Case Study: John

Dealing With Perfectionism

Real Life Case Study: Peter

Chapter Three – Changing Your Mindset

Blame it on your Lizard Brain

What's your Relationship with Time?

How to Realistically Declutter your Space

Making Positive Changes

Chapter Four – Easy Time Tracking & Analysis

Real Life Case Study: Chris

How to Easily Track your Time

Real Life Case Study: Joanne

Chapter Five – Increased Productivity and Better Time Management

Make your goals SMART

Real Life Case Study: Judith

Chapter Six – Prioritization – It's Easier Than You Think!

The Eisenhower Matrix

Eliminate, Automate, and Delegate

The 80/20 Rule (The Pareto Principle)

Decision Making

Real Life Case Study: Julia

Chapter 7 – Realistic Self-Care

How To Get Better Quality Sleep

Meditation – It's Not What You Think!

Nutrition Tips

Chapter 8 – Ending Procrastination Forever!

Overcoming Procrastination From Today!

Real Life Case Study: Dave

Chapter 9 – How To *Actually* Get and Keep Focus

The Key To Deep Focus

Importance of Flow and How to Trigger it

The Key To Eliminating Distractions

The Pomodoro Method

Real Life Case Study: Jane

Chapter 10 – Easy and Quick Productivity Helpers

Real Life Case Study: Linda

Get More Done In Life. Keep Calm. Be In Control.

It's Time To Solve The Procrastination Puzzle

Few resources are as precious and as limited as time. We live in a fast-paced world where every second counts. New opportunities and advances in technology are making our lives simultaneously easier and harder than they have ever been before.

Our days are filled with seemingly never-ending emails, meetings, blogs, books, newspapers to read, new skills to learn and new technology to keep abreast of. Added to that, owning a smartphone means you can easily get through a few more emails at home while commuting or even on holiday.

It's little wonder many of us feel overwhelmed and exhausted. We're living in an epidemic of 'busy,' and some of the technology that helps us be more productive is also fragmenting our focus. How many times have you picked up your smartphone 'just for a minute' to check your emails, and found yourself on Facebook an hour later, phone still in hand?

Everybody is busy. We're working more hours, commuting further distances, consuming more content, watching more television and learning more new skills. Time pressures and distractions are everywhere, and it can be overwhelming to know how to deal with them.

Poor time management doesn't just impact your work. It increases stress and can impact your health. The longer it continues, the more tired and frustrated you become as you try to keep on top of your never-ending to-do-list. Even your relationships can become strained when you don't have enough time to devote to the important people in your life.

Time management strategies can benefit anyone who feels like they can't fit enough into their day. Here are some examples of real people who could use the strategies in this book.

Real Life Case Study: Gayle

Gayle is an executive PA, whose team was recently downsized. She went from being responsible for one company executive to two, overnight. Her workload almost doubled, and while both her bosses understood it would take time for her to adjust, there were still a lot of tasks that needed urgent completion. To keep up, she increased the hours she was working, took work home with her and skipped lunch.

Before long she noticed her stress was building, and despite being hardworking and generally efficient, she's now struggling to keep on top of things. She is suffering from anxiety symptoms and beginning to make mistakes with simple tasks.

Real Life Case Study: Simon

Simon is a law student. His studies are intensive, and his goal is to graduate with honors and become a junior partner in a law firm.

Twice a week, Simon plays football for his college team. He also works two evenings a week, plus one weekend day, at a local fast food restaurant to pay off his student loans. He mostly manages to keep up with school work by pulling all-night study marathons on the nights he isn't working.

It's now his final year, and his increased workload means that he is really feeling the pressure. He can't afford to not work, and he enjoys playing football, but he feels like something has to give.

Real Life Case Study: Joseph

Joseph is an entrepreneur who works from home. He quit his corporate finance job to start a new coaching venture, and the flexibility of working from home appealed to him as he has a young family.

Building his business has been a struggle, and he often has to perform tasks that aren't his primary skill, such as closing new clients and developing a website. He fills most of his day with one-hour client calls and allows two hours for generating new leads and completing admin work. He'd like to have more time to work on his business, and not just in it, but that seems impossible at the minute.

In the early days, he finished work at 5 pm every day to help his wife with their three young children. Recently, as his business has grown, he's finding it more and more difficult to switch off. As his to-do list becomes longer, he's spending more and more time catching up with admin tasks and answering client emails out of hours.

In his coaching practice, he advises others on the importance of work-life balance, but he feels like a hypocrite as he isn't currently achieving that for himself.

Real Life Case Study: Serena

Serena is a stay at home mom, whose husband works for a

large accountancy firm. Her two children are 6 months, and 3 years old. When she first decided to be a stay at home mom, Serena imagined that she would spend her days playing and baking with the kids. Nap time would be spent cleaning the house, and her husband would come home each evening to a perfectly clean home and happy, relaxed wife. Perhaps, once the kids started preschool, she would take up a hobby or two, and join a gym.

The reality is less idyllic. Serena spends her days running errands, attending play dates, navigating fussy eating issues and handling toddler tantrums. If the children do nap she's too exhausted to clean the house. By the time her husband gets home, the house still isn't tidy, and Serena just wants to sleep.

Her husband is frustrated at the lack of quality time they get together, and Serena feels that she doesn't have enough time for herself. She barely has any energy left to keep up with the hobbies and regular exercise that she enjoyed before having two children. She feels almost permanently exhausted and craves enough time to do something for herself.

These are just a few real-life scenarios where time management techniques can have a real impact. Almost all of us experience a feeling that we don't have enough time on a frequent basis.

This book is to help you identify how to maximize the time you do have and get more done. We'll look at the reasons behind poor time management, and how some habits are time-stealers disguised as productivity boosters.

You'll understand why some people manage time better than others, the science and psychology behind getting organized and being effective and learn tools and strategies to start achieving more of your goals.

These strategies are suitable for anybody wanting to gain back control of their time. Whether you're a student, businessman, working mom or a homemaker, you'll find useful tools and techniques to implement. The vast majority of these can be adapted for any person, at any stage of their lives to make the most of the 24 hours we all get in a day.

There are no one-size-fits-all solutions to time management, but with the tips and techniques outlined in this book you will be able to:

- Identify where your time should be spent
- Learn how to work smarter, **not harder**
- Tackle procrastination head-on with easy techniques
- Delegate or outsource the right tasks
- Make time for the things that matter to you
- Enjoy a *true* work-life balance.

By applying the proven time management strategies laid out in the following chapters, you will be able to take back control over your time and get more done.

Chapter One – Effective Time Management

"Dost thou love life? Then do not squander time, for that's the stuff life is made of."
Benjamin Franklin.

A Brief History of Time Management
In many ways, mankind has always been seeking to understand and control time. Even prehistoric man understood time in the sense of the time between sunrise and sunset, the changing seasons, and the most effective times to hunt, farm or migrate.

Our more modern concept of time management and efficiency stems from the time of industrial revolution, and the roots of modern time management originate from business. During this time, the concept of productivity was defined. Advances like assembly lines and shift work allowed for higher production rates of physical goods.

We opened this chapter with a quote from Benjamin Franklin, who is widely considered as the father of modern time management. He developed many of the common time management strategies we still utilize today, with an emphasis on planning, efficiency and working hard to get the job done. He strongly believed in efficiency as a benchmark for personal and professional goals. Many of our common sayings about time stem from Benjamin Franklin quotes, including the ubiquitous "Time is money."

In 1888, Willard Bundy was one of the first inventors to create a mechanical time recording device, The Bundy Key Recorder. It helped businesses keep track of their employees' hours. This device made tracking the hours that employees worked much easier, and businesses began to monitor punctuality and demand efficiency.

In 1911 Frederick Winslow Taylor published, *"The Principles of Scientific Management"*. His theory of management became known as **Taylorism** and was based on creating workflows. The main objective was to improve worker productivity by finding the best practice way of completing a task and training all employees to complete it that way.

Taylorism focused predominantly on factory workers, and so in 1954, Peter Drucker created the concept of management by objectives in his publication, *"The Practice of Management"*. He stressed that to manage a business effectively, you need to balance a variety of needs and goals, rather than measuring just one metric.

In all, Drucker wrote 39 books and accurately predicted many of the business developments of the late 20th century, including the emergence of the information society.

As the world of business continued to progress, time management and efficiency became increasingly important. James McKay published the first book relating solely to the art of time management, *"The Management of Time"*, in 1959.

Fast forward to today, and time management is still a hot topic. Despite the influx of technology designed to streamline and simplify our lives, our need for effective solutions to manage our time is only growing.

Why Do We Need Time Management?
Do you ever feel like there are not enough hours in a day?

You work hard, you're busy all day long, yet at the end of the day, you still haven't finished everything you hoped to achieve. That longed-for sense of satisfaction eludes you. Or no matter how well you plan your days, or how disciplined you try to be, something unexpected happens and boom! Your whole day and your carefully laid plans go completely awry.

Tired and frustrated, you write tomorrow's to-do- list and hope there are fewer setbacks and distractions so that you can manage your time better. Yet, once again despite your good intentions, you find yourself exhausted at the end of the day, with a dozen outstanding or half-completed tasks on your to-do list.

If so, you're not alone. Many of us reach the end of the day without achieving everything on our to-do lists. Those glorious days where things go to plan – or we manage to successfully handle the distractions and still get it all done, are few and far between.

If this sounds like you, chances are you need some time management techniques to help you gain back control of your time. Good time management skills will help you get more done, with less stress, and move you closer to your goals each day.

Applying the techniques outlined in this book will help you become more effective, and end more of your days feeling accomplished, not exhausted.

Why is it so Hard to Manage Time?
We talk about 'time management' a lot, but in reality, it's not time we're managing. We're managing ourselves and our tasks. The 24 hours in a day that we all get will pass at

the same rate of minutes and seconds, no matter what. We can't manage the passage of time, only what we do with it.

Sometimes we mistake great time management for being busy all the time. We fill our days and our lives with constant activity, and even if we do miraculously manage to keep on top of it all, we risk burnout.

You might look at other people who seem to be fitting everything in and wonder how on earth they manage it. Perhaps you think they just work 'faster' than you do, or that they are 'naturally' always busy.

The surprising truth is that it's not always the fastest or the busiest workers that are the most effective, as demonstrated by this tale of two administrators.

Louise and Mandy were both in line for an upcoming promotion to a management position. The hiring manager was very keen on hiring the person who was most productive and would be monitoring them both for two weeks.

Mandy had always been the fastest worker and a keen multi-tasker. She thought she'd be a shoe-in for the position. By the time Louise had written one report, Mandy could have written two and answered all her incoming emails. She prided herself on always being busy and getting things done fast.

However, Louise took the slow but steady approach. She kept a comprehensive 'to do' list that held all her key tasks for the day, week and month. She reviewed the tasks and placed them in order of priority. If there were tasks that could be easily delegated to the office intern and still be done to the right standard, she would delegate those tasks.

She also knew that she was most productive during the morning, until after eating lunch. She worked on the most mentally challenging and important tasks in the mornings, saving less important tasks for the afternoon.

In contrast, Mandy flitted from one task to another, taking pride in picking up other people's work. She felt important for being the person that never said 'no.' She didn't see the need to delegate and she multi-tasked as though her life depended on it.

Unfortunately, Mandy was so fixated on being busy that she began to take longer to complete a task. While she was working on numerous tasks, many were still only half-finished by the end of a day. While Mandy was chasing her tail trying to immediately respond to all her emails and chasing up the extra work she'd taken on, Louise had set up an automated response. Instead of having to immediately reply, each person would be automatically informed that their email had been received and would be answered within two hours.

Louise stuck to her 'to do' list as her guide. She made sure that each task was finished before she moved on to the next, never multi-tasking or allowing distractions to break her focus. She planned her day and stuck to allocated times for responding to emails and phone calls.

By the end of the two weeks, Mandy began to realize that while she had been busy the whole time, only half of her tasks were actually completed. In fact, some important tasks were now dangerously close to the deadline.

When the hiring manager reviewed both ladies work, Louise had consistently met targets and produced high-quality work, where Mandy had missed two deadlines and made mistakes in some projects.

The moral of the story? Time management is an important skill which anyone can master. With the right tools and systems in place, you can get everything on your to-do list done. Both Mandy and Louise had the same amount of time and tasks, yet their approaches were vastly different.

Where Mandy fell into the trap of constant activity and trying to simply go faster, Louise was able to put systems in place that made sure she freed up her own time to concentrate on the right things. The real aim of managing your time is not to do more, it's to do more of the right things.

Why is it so Hard to get Everything Done?
We live in an age where we are bombarded with communication, wherever we are. If you own a smartphone, you are almost always connected to the world, via social media, news alerts, emails, phone calls and text messages. You can receive mobile signals in some of the most remote places, and we often believe that we need to be, or should be, connected 24/7.

Yet, not so long ago, once you left the house, you weren't contactable until you reached a building with a telephone. If you were at a computer, you might have email access, but you weren't expected to respond immediately, or be available and connected 24/7.

All of these constant communications lead us to be distracted multiple times in a day. Often, we turn to multi-tasking, and we will even pride ourselves on how many tasks we can perform at one time. Except that the productivity boost we think we get with multi-tasking is mostly an illusion. We'll explore the myth of multi-tasking in a later chapter.

Social media and the internet provide opportunities that were impossible for most people only 25 years ago. You can run a business entirely from home via the internet. You can easily research or learn almost anything. You can make friends in far-flung continents you've never visited and speak to them in real-time via video calls. You can reconnect with long-lost friends, share pictures of your kids with family across the world, and make informed purchasing decisions by reading customer reviews.

It's incredible, but it's also a huge time drain if you let it be. I'd be willing to bet that there's nobody reading this book who hasn't fallen down an internet rabbit hole at one time or another, if not daily!

It starts innocuously enough, you're just going to answer that message from Aunt Margaret via Facebook. Before you know it, half an hour has passed, with you scrolling through your Facebook feed. You know what everyone ate for dinner yesterday, the funniest things your friend's children said, and you've watched six cat videos. Unfortunately, you still haven't answered Aunt Margaret.

Or, you go to research a large electrical purchase. You go to the major retailers and consumer review websites and look for the best options. You get a good idea of what you want to buy based on your budget and the information available to you.

It's now three hours later, and you're on your fourteenth YouTube video. It started with video reviews of the product you're buying, but now you're just watching videos of people playing hilarious pranks on each other, or adorable cats, again!

Allowing distractions, procrastinating, and overworking are all things that are eating away at your potential to achieve your goals.

Even if you diligently avoid the perils of social media and the internet, you're not alone if you find that you still end the day frazzled and worn-out, without achieving what you set out to achieve. We live in a culture where working hard is valued, and working long hours is synonymous with working hard. Perhaps you think that if you're not frazzled after a day's work, then you're not working hard enough?

The problem is, you're actually negatively impacting your health by overworking. Added to that, you're also negatively impacting your own productivity by working longer hours and pushing yourself to get more done.

What Happens when you don't Manage your Time Effectively?

When you're not managing your time effectively, you'll start to experience negative effects that go beyond poor productivity. Your stress levels increase as you think of your growing and never-ending task list. It begins to look like a mountain of work that could be impossible to climb, so you begin to procrastinate more.

To make up for your procrastination time, you start to try and work harder, or rush work, leading to low-quality work, more stress, and exhaustion. Guilt about your procrastinating creeps in and you start to mentally 'beat yourself up.' Why can't you just be more efficient? Why didn't you tackle your tasks sooner?

You start to wonder about your job security and if your boss thinks you are efficient enough. You put in more hours. You have less time for self-care or spending with family. Yet you still don't manage to complete all of your tasks.

The good news is that you can take back control. You can achieve the things you want to achieve, and still have time to sleep and socialize, or spend time with your family. Even better, the answer isn't a series of extreme or complicated 'life hacks', like taking several naps a day instead of sleep or getting up at 5 am each day.

You can make real and lasting changes that enable you to manage your time more effectively in a sustainable way. No quick fixes, just real and measurable results. While there are no one-size fits all cure, this book looks at helping you identify your time drains and blind spots. And it offers practical, realistic advice to solve them.

The techniques outlined in this book work, and they work very well. As long as you put the effort in to make the changes and implement the techniques, you will see an increase in your productivity.

Where are You now – and Where do You need to be?
In order to make those changes, you'll need to review where you are now with your time management. It's important to be honest with yourself about how you currently use your time, and what you really want to achieve with the time you have.

Self-awareness will help you identify and address issues much quicker, and not being honest with yourself will only sabotage your efforts. Sometimes, we're actually quite aware of how and why we aren't achieving enough, and yet we bury our heads in the sand instead of addressing it head-on.

It's also important to be aware of your strengths, to know what to capitalize on and where to focus your efforts. The better you understand your goals and motivations, strengths and weaknesses, the easier it is to manage your time effectively.

Know your own time management style and any areas where you fall down. Do you procrastinate? Do you write a to-do list and then ignore it? Do you have trouble saying no to things that interrupt your day? Knowing yourself allows you to see clearly where you need to focus your efforts and is an important first step to making effective change happen.

Successfully developing time management skills requires that you examine your existing values and priorities and make changes to your lifestyle accordingly. It's not always easy, but the potential benefits of decreased stress, higher achievements and improved personal relationships are certainly worth the effort.

Where You Need To Be

Answer these questions honestly:
- What strategies do you use now to manage your time?
- How effective are the strategies you use now?
- What are your worst 'bad habits' when it comes to how you use your time?
- How committed are you to implementing change?

Write the answers down and be as honest with yourself as you can be. We'll be referring back to these throughout the book, so keep the answers handy to refer back to.

Time is like money. Spend it wisely, and invest a little and you will reap the rewards. Squander it, and while it might provide some instant gratification, you will be poorer for it in the future. Now, we're not talking about spending every minute you have in a fully productive state. That wouldn't be wise either. But balance and an honest approach to what is really beneficial when it comes to how you spend your time are essential to getting the most out of it.

Now that we've looked at the background of time management, you understand that the key to effectively getting more done is to build the right, sustainable habits. Some of this will involve unlearning some old, unhelpful habits. You may have implemented some of these in the hopes of improving your time management, only to find them unhelpful, or even worse – time drains themselves.

Unfortunately, there are some things which appear on the surface to be wise investments but actually turn out to be time drains. In Chapter Two, we'll identify some common false friends when it comes to time management.

Chapter Two – The Productivity Factors

"The way we measure productivity is flawed. People checking their BlackBerry over dinner is not the measure of productivity."
Tim Ferriss.

In the quest for great time management, many of us will try numerous techniques and technologies, searching for that perfect fix or 'life hack' that makes us more productive.

Unfortunately, there are many practices and habits that people pick up in the hope of improving their output that turn out to be false friends. These sabotaging habits eventually eat away at the productive time you have. In this chapter, we'll take a look at some of the practices that might be sabotaging your efforts to manage your time. We'll examine them in greater depth in later chapters, but it's important to understand early on in your time management journey what and why these practices are unhelpful.

Multitasking

One of the most insidious false friends is multitasking. It's something we often consider as necessary, especially if we're busy. Most of us at some time or another have multi-tasked or at least attempted to. The idea is that by being able to work on more than one task simultaneously, you'll get more done in less time.

Mothers are notorious for being consummate multitaskers, handling a variety of tasks at any one time. In some situations, like dealing with a demanding toddler while needing to get anything at all done, it's unavoidable.

For many years people have worked on their multitasking skills hoping to achieve the holy grail of productivity. For entrepreneurs and time-pressed managers, multitasking seems like a dream come true in a hectic life. Unfortunately, the reality of multitasking is quite the opposite.

If you believe yourself to be the exception to the rule, think again. One study by *Stanford* University showed that participants who believed they were excellent multitaskers, actually made more mistakes, recalled fewer details, and took longer to finish tasks than those who did not identify as multitaskers.

Numerous studies have proven that multitasking is a myth and that our brains cannot effectively handle more than one task at a time. By distracting yourself constantly between two or more tasks, you are fragmenting your focus. Your brain takes time to switch from one job to the other. Instead of making it quicker, completing the two tasks simultaneously will take longer than simply doing one task at a time, giving each your full attention. One study showed that this kind of start-stop approach on several tasks can increase the time it takes to complete those tasks by 500%!

The evidence against multitasking is compelling. If you focus on one thing at a time, not only will you be faster, but you will produce higher quality work.

Real Life Case Study: John

John is a business analyst who identifies as a multi-tasker. He believes that by doing two or three things at once he is getting more done. In reality, his projects are often rushed because he is trying to do too much at once. When asked why he feels multitasking is the best way of working, he explains that he feels bored completing one thing at a time and enjoys having several things going on at once.

John feels that his best work is completed when he is under pressure, and that his work is of a better standard when it is completed close to the deadline. Despite believing that he works best this way, he is beginning to display symptoms of stress because of the constant time pressure he puts himself under. It's also beginning to be noted by his manager that although his work is of a reasonable standard, mistakes are beginning to creep in.

It's likely that John's work actually suffers from his multitasking and last-minute approach, rather than being enhanced by it. A more balanced approach would be better for his health and potentially produce more accurate work.

It's not always possible to avoid multitasking, especially as a parent. You might need to cook dinner while helping a child with their homework, or you might be listening to an audiobook while driving. These are relatively mild multitasking attempts but for important tasks, or when you have a very long to-do list, you should aim to focus on one task at a time.

What really improves productivity is the opposite of multitasking. If you think about the last time you finished the day feeling accomplished, you most likely weren't doing much multitasking at all. In fact, you were probably focusing on one task at a time and giving it your full attention before moving on to the next one. Rather than multitasking, you were single-tasking and achieving a deep focus.

Single-tasking is its own skill set. In 2010, two Harvard psychologists discovered that 47% of our time is spent thinking about something completely unrelated to what we're doing. The implications to your productivity are huge. Being attentive most of the time is going to allow you to complete more tasks than someone who can only concentrate on the task at hand for 50% of the time.

Even better, the more you practice single-tasking, the better you become at it. It's a skill that, like any other, gets better with practice. So, if you are easily distracted, it is possible to train your brain to concentrate for longer periods of time. And in turn, you will naturally become more productive.

Working Longer Hours
The second false friend, working longer hours, is also a common trap that people fall into when faced with high workloads. Like multitasking, it seems to be the answer to your problem. While it's true that simply working overtime very occasionally can have some benefits, as a regular practice it will cause more harm than you think.
If you can't fit everything you need to do into your day, it seems like a no-brainer to try to spend more time to get those things done. You might work through your lunch, stay late at the office instead of going to the gym or socializing, or go to bed a little later. It seems like a great way to cross more things off your to-do list.

Working more hours can increase your productivity in the short term. And if unplanned things occasionally crop up, it's not always a bad interim strategy to get back on track. But if you find yourself regularly stealing time from other essential activities to dedicate to your work, then it's time to reassess. Chances are, it worked well at first, but now you find yourself in a vicious circle. You're working longer and longer hours to keep up- until you literally run out of time.

Some workplaces have a culture where working long hours is seen as a valuable trait in an employee. In this kind of culture, working long hours is seen as synonymous with working hard and getting a lot done. It may be expected that anyone who wants to succeed will put in long hours to show their commitment to the company. Luckily, this kind of culture is becoming less and less popular as more evidence is coming to light that indicates that working long hours can have the opposite effect.

One reason that merely working longer hours provides diminishing returns is because it increases your stress levels and impacts your health. Being truly productive requires you to be healthy, both physically and mentally. The toll that long working hours takes on your body is counter-productive to achieving your goals.

You can literally work yourself to death. According to a study from The University College London, people who work longer than 7-8 hours a day increase their risk of heart disease by a shocking 67%. While long hours are surely not the only factor, you should certainly think twice before you get into a habit of working long hours on a regular basis.

Great time management recognizes that you need balance in your life. The ratios may be a little different from person to person, but you should give the same importance to rest, relaxation and social time that you do to work time. While it can seem like spending your precious time on activities that aren't productive is a 'waste,' you'll find that the time you spend recharging allows you to get a lot more done during productive times.

There are occasional exceptions. If an emergency crops up,

you might need to adjust your balance, but this should be very short term. If you find 'emergencies' creeping in regularly, then you also need to reassess how you deal with them and identify the root cause. If you have clients or a boss that makes unreasonable demands, then you may need to have a conversation with them to set expectations.

If you're reading this and wondering how you can get everything done without working a few extra hours, don't worry. We'll be looking at lots of techniques for maximizing the time you spend working so that long hours become a thing of the past.

Dealing With Perfectionism

Often given as a glib answer to the common interview question, perfectionism is, often, a weakness. Yet it's a weakness that we're proud to have and one we wear like a badge of honor. We see perfectionism as a positive because it means we are committed to producing quality.

Perfectionists don't let shoddy work slide and can be trusted to complete a job to the highest of standards. There are some circumstances where perfectionism can come in handy and are a neccessity. If you're a proofreader, you'll want to make sure a document is perfect before sending it back to the author. If you're an architect, you'll want to make sure your buildings are perfectly designed for their function. But you can take perfectionism too far.

For one, what does 'perfect' really mean? It's a subjective standard for most occupations and an unattainable goal in most circumstances. Perfectionism can drive you to work on a task well beyond the point where the extra effort is adding any real value.

The time you spend trying to make your work perfect when

it's already good enough is a waste of time and energy that could be spent on more valuable tasks. This doesn't mean that you should only complete tasks to a 'reasonable' standard, or that quality isn't important. The standard to which you complete each task should be relative to its purpose and importance.

For example, when you create a presentation, the key outcome is that it looks professional, prompts the presenter at the right places and backs up the information they are delivering. A simple format with bullet points and the occasional graph or visual is usually enough. If it takes you three days to create, and two of those are adding various animations and frills, then it's almost certainly time spent better doing something else.

There may be times when those details are necessary to pay attention to, but for the majority of tasks, done is better than perfect. It's important to be honest with yourself about what standard is required for each task and not allow yourself to go overboard. Anything you do should really be adding value to the project. Once your actions aren't adding value, it's time to focus on the next task or project.

Perfectionism can also cause you to procrastinate. When you doubt your ability to do a job to the extreme high standards that you expect of yourself, you may begin to avoid doing that task at all.

Getting things done to a high standard is commendable, but when perfectionism prevents you from moving on to other important tasks, or means you miss deadlines because of procrastination, it becomes a real problem.

Dedication to high-quality work is admirable, but remember to keep the overall goal and the importance of the task in mind. If you notice that you are spending too long on one task trying to make it perfect, make an effort to move on as soon as you have completed it to a reasonable standard. This will horrify staunch perfectionists, but it's true: In most cases, good enough really is good enough.

Your Smartphone and Social Media

The invention of smartphones has made it much easier for busy people to stay in touch with their work and accomplish tasks on the go.

You can now not only take calls, send messages and check your email from almost anywhere, but you can also download apps for virtually any purpose.

There are study apps, word processors, spreadsheets and presentation creation apps, as well as mobile versions of project software, billing and invoicing apps, graphic design apps, and even time management apps! The list is almost endless.

While there are many benefits to being able to work from your smartphone, we tend to use our phones for many purposes. We keep up to date with friends and family via social media, play games in our recreation time, do our shopping, and even read books on our phones. This reliance on our phones for all areas of our lives can blur the boundaries between work and recreation time.

Although they are indeed useful tools, our over reliance on our smartphones can mean that they become a big distraction. According to one market research company, Americans touch their phones over 2,000 times a day on average, and a 2016 study showed that more than a third of people check their phone within five minutes of waking up.

Social media plays a large part in most people's addictions to their smartphones. It's no longer unusual to see diners taking pictures of their lunch to post to Facebook or Instagram. You can lose hours in a debate on Twitter, and Pinterest can be both a useful research tool for tasks such as home improvement projects, and an enormous time drain.

Social media also provides instant gratification. Studies have shown that it impacts parts of the brain in a similar way to drug use, which is what makes it so addictive. While moderate users of social media don't see any adverse effects, heavy users of social media can experience increased anxiety and irritability. We're not suggesting you stop using social media by any stretch of the imagination. But if you find it difficult to go for long periods without checking your feeds, it could be a sign that you need to limit your social media time in order to regain some productivity.

Our habit of regularly checking our phones is also switching our brains into constant multi-task mode. When you pause what you're doing to check that notification or have a quick look at Facebook, you're switching tasks rapidly. Doing this kind of rapid switching multiple times in a day is hurting your brain's ability to focus for extended periods.

Our reliance on smartphones makes us crave the distraction they provide. People who use their phones regularly will often found themselves reaching for their phone while waiting at a bus stop, or even while walking down the street. To compound the issue, checking your phone constantly can cause you to have higher stress levels than people who limit their smartphone use. The added stress impairs your ability to concentrate, compounding the issue even more.

It's not just social media that causes the distraction issues. News services, checking your email, and any app that sends regular notifications to your phone can all become distractions from more important tasks at hand.

You don't need to throw your smartphone away or swear off all technology to regain your productivity, but you do need to become mindful of how, and when, you are using your phone. Try to limit your phone use to certain times of the day if possible. When you have a task to focus on, lock your phone in a drawer or turn it off to minimize distractions.

Here's an example of an entrepreneur who realized his smartphone use was hindering his productivity, and took steps to address the issue:

Real Life Case Study: Peter

Peter, a digital marketing consultant, started his own business after twelve years in a corporate environment. Moving from a large company with many employees to working on his own meant that he was no longer surrounded by colleagues or spending large amounts of time in meetings.

He was looking forward to getting more done with less distraction.

Peter planned to use social networks like Facebook and LinkedIn to grow his business and generate leads. Yet after three months, he noticed that more and more, he was using his phone to interact socially on those platforms instead of generating leads.

While there was still benefit in using the platforms to grow his business, he recognized that he was spending too much time on social platforms. Worst of all, it was detracting from his ability to complete other necessary tasks for his business.

He decided to take action. He purchased a basic phone with no internet capability so that he could still receive business related calls on the go and switched his smartphone off for a minimum of 6 hours a day. He also outsourced some of his business related social media activities so that he could avoid falling into the same trap on his desktop.

The result was that he managed to achieve a deeper focus during his workdays. Work on client projects was wrapped up in a much shorter timeframe, allowing Peter ample time to service the new leads being generated from his outsourced social media.

These are just a few of the false friends and time saboteurs that we all encounter on a day-to-day basis. Some are easier than others to avoid, and some of them, like perfectionism, are ingrained into our perception of who we are.

Go back to the questions you answered in **Chapter One** and look at your answer to question three: What are your worst 'bad habits' when it comes to how you use your time?

Do you have any new ones to add to the list now?

To overcome all of these bad habits, it's essential that we develop the right mindset to support our new, more productive habits. We'll take a look at how to adjust your time mindset in Chapter Three.

Chapter Three – Changing Your Mindset

"The butterfly counts not months but moments, and has time enough."
Rabindranath Tagor.

We've touched briefly in previous chapters upon the concept that managing your time is less about time itself and more about managing yourself. Your mindset plays an important part in how successful your attempts at time management will be. Your mindset can also influence numerous success factors in your life, beyond time management.

So, how does mindset impact your time management, specifically? First, to be in the right frame of mind to manage your time, you need to understand your motivations. Nobody wants to be more productive for the simple joy of being productive. For you to spend time and energy on a task, there needs to be a reason, plus a determination to achieve your end goal.

If you don't have specific goals, then you need to set some. We'll look at goal setting in more detail in Chapter 5, but you need clear and realistic goals, and a plan to achieve them. If you know what your goals are, the purpose of managing your time should be to move you closer to achieving those goals. Without goals, you won't be able to manage your time.

Sometimes, we know exactly what our goals are and yet something holds us back from achieving them. We procrastinate, prioritize unimportant tasks and come up with endless reasons why we can't do something. We often blame lack of time for this lack of achievement, but the reality is that we're holding ourselves back.

When you have unachieved goals that you find yourself blaming time for, take a look inside yourself and see if you might be holding yourself back. It sounds ridiculous, but sometimes our own fears and beliefs are what stands between us and our goals. We know what we need to do, but we resist taking action towards our goals. Often this is because not achieving it fulfills some psychological need we may not even be aware of.

Blame it on your Lizard Brain

Dr. Paul MacLean, an American physician and neuroscientist, divided the brain into three main sections. The first of these is commonly referred to as the reptilian brain, or lizard brain.

Your lizard brain controls your involuntary functions: breathing, your heartbeat, perspiration. This part of your brain is also in charge of your survival, managing your *'fight or flight'* responses, and how you experience fear. It's this aspect of the lizard brain, processing fear, that causes it to hold you back from achieving everything you are capable of.

In today's world, we don't often come across true life or death situations, but the lizard brain analyzes everything through its primitive filter. Every task and action is being weighed up to determine: will this keep you safe, or is it dangerous?

The lizard brain's concept of dangerous is pretty unsophisticated, and it will often fear things that would benefit you in the long term. It's strange but true that many of us are actually afraid of success. Or, perhaps more accurately, our lizard brains are afraid of success.

Achieving goals makes you successful. Being successful makes you stand out, and for your lizard brain, that makes you attractive to predators. Your lizard brain still works in much the same way it has done for thousands of years. The fact that you're not being hunted by predators doesn't deter it from doing its job.

It's not only success that your lizard brain wants to protect you from. Failing could harm your self-esteem, and your lizard brain doesn't want you to deal with the pain of discovering that you are incapable of achieving your dreams. It will convince you to not make the effort and make it easy for you to blame time or something else instead of risking the failure.

Your lizard brain is easily frightened. It wants to keep you where you are. Where you are is safe even if it's not where you want to be. If you take action towards big, life-changing goals, you risk either succeeding or failing, and both of those are undesirable. So, it comes up with reasons, excuses, ways to prevent you from getting there. Your insistence that you don't have enough time is probably rooted in fear and driven by your lizard brain.

When you find yourself making excuses, and just not getting something done, you need to identify what exactly is holding you back. Identifying the problem can be harder than it sounds. These self-imposed resistances are often well-disguised and can be tricky to get the bottom of. Look out for the tasks that you put off the most even though they would drive you closer to your goals, and then try to identify why. I promise you, it's probably not lack of time!

What's your Relationship with Time?

Let's do a quick exercise to identify your current relationship with time. How many of these phrases have you used in the last week?

- I'm so busy
- I'm too busy
- There's just not enough time
- I don't have time
- If I just had more time
- There's not enough hours in the day

When you dissect them and break them down, these common phrases mean more than appears on the surface. Let's dissect them and see what you're really saying when you use them.

I'm too busy, I don't have time.
This is usually used as a way to decline a request or an invitation. What you are really saying is that's not a priority. When you consider the recent occasions where you have said 'I'm too busy' would you have been comfortable saying instead 'that's not a priority'? Or even, 'you're not a priority'? Sounds harsher, doesn't it?

Consider Serena, who we met in the introduction. She's a busy mom of two. If her three-year-old daughter asked her to play outside with her, she would think nothing of saying 'I can't honey, I'm too busy.' Yet she might hesitate to say 'I can't honey, you're not my priority right now.' It would sound terrible. Yet that's effectively what she's saying when she tells her daughter she's too busy.

There's no shame in not prioritizing other people's needs

over your own. If Serena was cooking dinner for the family, then playing outside with her daughter would, justifiably, not be her priority. If she was folding laundry that could be done another time, she might feel differently if she recognized the message that she was really giving.

If you're saying 'I don't have time' to do things that you do consider a priority, you should probably be working on your prioritization skills ASAP.

There's just not enough time, if I just had more time, there's not enough hours in a day.
There are 24 hours in a day, and 168 hours in a week. Time is finite, but you do have enough of it to achieve anything that anyone in history has ever achieved and more. We all get the same amount of time. If you can't get enough done in the same amount of time granted to all of us, you are either overstretching yourself and trying to do too much or not concentrating on the right things. It's probably the latter!

I'm so busy.
This is used in a few different ways. It can be used as a precursor to refusing a request or an invitation to do something, as mentioned. However, it can also be a way of making ourselves feel important. If we're busy, then we must be busy doing important things, right? Busyness can also be used as a kind of competition. How often do you find yourself comparing with a friend or an acquaintance about how busy you both are? It might even descend into a conversation about how stressed you both are.

We wear busy like it's a badge of honor, but it's not impressing anyone. We're all busy. The really impressive people are the ones who we know take big actions, get results, move closer to their goals every day and yet never complain about being busy. If you ask them how they are, they'll respond with a big grin and say "Great!"

Now consider how you speak about your own time management skills. Even if it's just your own thoughts that you don't say out loud, those words have power over you. How often do you say or think the following:

- I'm lazy
- I'm too disorganized
- I never have enough time
- I'm too slow

These kinds of phrases are part of what we call self-limiting beliefs. They are ideas that you have about the way the world works, the person you are and your own capabilities and they are often false. They're also incredibly addictive, and they keep us in that cycle of not achieving enough.

Think about it, what are the consequences of continually telling yourself that you don't have enough time, or that you're disorganized? It's a self-fulfilling prophecy. You will constantly feel under time pressure and stressed out. You begin to believe it so strongly that it becomes your main excuse for not fulfilling responsibilities or meeting deadlines.

This idea that you don't have enough time is part of a scarcity mindset. To get the most out of your time, you will need to replace it with an abundance mindset. To do that, you need to change the way you think about time. How do you change your thoughts? By changing the words you use. Replace your negative phrases and self-talk with positive ones.

A useful tip is to use the Neuro Linguistic programming

method of re-framing. Instead of 'I'm so busy' re-frame it as 'I have a lot of things I'd like to achieve today.' Look for a positive way to view situations and avoid using negative words in relation to time. The more you use words of abundance instead of lack when you discuss time, the less overwhelmed you will feel, and the more you will achieve.

While it won't magically create more time, changing the way you think and speak about time can make a surprising amount of difference. It helps you bypass your lizard brain and subconsciously sets you up to succeed.

Perfectionism
One issue we can face that holds us back is perfectionism. We discussed this briefly in the previous chapter where we looked at how perfectionism can cause you to spend more time than necessary on a task. Yet that's not the only damaging effect of perfectionism. It can also prevent you from getting started or completing a task.

For perfectionists, the fear of not being able to complete the task to the standard they expect of themselves causes the issue. It can cause perfectionists to overrun on deadlines, trying desperately to get it 'just right,' or even worse, fear of failure keeps them from even starting.

If you suffer from perfectionistic tendencies, here are some ways to overcome that:

- Set a finite deadline for when a project must be finished and then quit working on the project when that deadline arrives.

- On an unimportant task, deliberately make it imperfect. Allow a typo to slip through in a Facebook status, don't line up the tins straight in your cupboards, wear socks that don't match. Once you see how nothing bad will happen, it can help you overcome your fear of imperfection.

- For more important tasks, set a clear goal and clear, achievable standards for the end outcome. Once you meet those standards, finish the project. Don't allow yourself to attempt to make it even better or add further requirements as you go.

- If you're overwhelmed by a large, important project and it's causing you to put off starting the project, break down the project into small and manageable chunks.

Perfectionism can be paralyzing. Make a decision now to not allow your perfectionism to hold you hostage. When faced with a task, do your best to put your perfectionist tendencies aside and get to work! Break it into small, manageable steps or just go gung-ho, as long as you are taking steps towards your goal it doesn't matter.

If you don't achieve exactly what you intended, then be proud that you did achieve something. You completed a task that might otherwise have been delayed endlessly while you grappled with doubt and procrastinated. Instead, you tackled it and now have the opportunity to learn and improve. Our greatest breakthroughs and achievements often come right on the back of failures so don't rob yourself of that chance to improve!

How to Realistically Declutter your Space

Another way to get into a positive headspace and reduce overwhelm is to declutter and minimize your working space. Clutter in the home or your working space can mean that you waste time looking for items, and just being in a messy environment can impact on your productivity and motivation to complete a task.

Having a good declutter can help you get more organized and feel less stressed. Use this checklist to help you decide what to keep and what to remove:

- Is this in full working order? Many of us keep an assortment of items that we honestly believe we will repair at some point. Yet we often never get around to it. If you've been hoarding broken or incomplete items, now is the time to throw them away.

- When was the last time I used or needed this? If it was more than a year ago and it's not a specialist item like a power tool, then it's probably time to dump it. Be ruthless!

- Is this valuable? Monetary or sentimentally. An item having monetary value doesn't mean you must keep it. If you no longer use the item, consider selling it.

Organize items into things that can be recycled, donated to charity shops, sold, papers to be shredded, and items that will simply need to be thrown away. If possible, clear them as soon as they are organized. Take them to the charity shop or list them on an auction site. Do it as soon as you can, take whatever action you need to ensure they are gone.

Once you've removed all unnecessary items, you need to make sure what is left is well organized and that you have adequate storage. If you don't have enough storage room, go back through and be even more ruthless with what you discard.

If you have a lot of papers in your workspace, or for

household finances, then make sure that these are meticulously organized into a filing system. Having papers scattered on your desk can hold you back from getting things done because it makes you feel disorganized.

Added to that, if you work from home, it's likely that your office is more than just an office. It's common for people to use their home office for extra storage but this can actually reduce your productivity.

Whether you work from home, or in a more formal environment, take time at the end of each day to clear up your working space. Make sure that your desk and the floor space around you are clear before you leave for the day. Return files and folders to their appropriate location.

Don't forget to organize and declutter your digital workspace too. Spend some time regularly clearing out and organizing files and folders on your PC or laptop and clear out unused or unnecessary apps from your smartphone and other devices. Doing this will make it easier to find the files, documents, and apps you need quickly.

Spend your Gap Time Wisely
We all dream of long, luxurious holidays on tropical beaches where we can laze around and do nothing all day. There's nothing wrong with that, and a good restful holiday can really recharge you when you're feeling a little burnt out.

In fact, it's imperative that we all take some time for rest and relaxation; but being idle for too long could actually make you miserable. Research conducted by the University of Chicago indicates that busy people are happier than people who indulge in idle activity.

As with everything, striking a balance is important. Studies have also shown that chocolate is good for you, but when you dive deeper into the research, it's limited to the very dark kind of chocolate. That large bar of delicious milk chocolate that is loaded with sugar is not helping your health.

In the same way, there's a difference between being stressed and overworked, and filling your time with meaningful activity. It doesn't have to be 'change the world' meaningful, it just has to be moving you closer to your goal, or something that you love doing.

If you're thinking that you love lying on the sofa and watching Netflix, we can empathize - but in the long run, that won't make you happy. Taking an afternoon to relax and do just that wouldn't hurt, and might help your short-term happiness, but a month of doing that? You'd be bored, and start craving meaningful work.

Being 'busy' doesn't have to be draining, either. Going on a hike, reading a book, gardening. These are all things that might relax and recharge you but are also not being idle. To tie this in with great time management, make sure you use your 'gap time' for fulfilling pursuits wherever possible. Learn a new skill, read that book you've had gathering dust on your bedside table, visit an art gallery. If it motivates or inspires you, then it's something worth making time for.

Making Positive Changes

Morgan is a history graduate who started to feel the pressure of studying in her final year. She wanted to go on to postgraduate study and needed to achieve good grades to be accepted to her ideal course. As a perfectionist, Morgan aimed for the highest possible grades on all of her assignments and always achieved them.

Unfortunately, halfway through the year, a bout of stomach flu wiped her out for almost two weeks. When she recovered, it seemed impossible to catch up on what she had missed. When her tutors asked her how she was doing, she responded with "I don't have enough time to catch up," or "I'm so stressed, I have so much to do and not enough time."

One of her tutors surprised her by suggesting that if she believed she'd never catch up, then she'd never catch up. He asked her to re-frame the situation in a more positive light. After some thought, Morgan re-framed the situation as "It's going to be a challenge to catch up with all the work I missed." Her tutor agreed, and they discussed why it was important to catch up, and what positive steps Morgan had taken so far.

Morgan was embarrassed to admit that she'd not taken any real positive action. Instead, she'd been paralyzed by fear of failure and allowed herself to be overwhelmed. There was no way she could put in enough time to receive a perfect grade, and so her perfectionism was keeping her frozen and doing nothing at all. Her tutor encouraged her to create a manageable plan to get back on track, incorporating some downtime.

Morgan had to accept that in this instance, it was more important to complete her outstanding assignments and receive a grade that was 'good enough' to get her accepted onto her postgraduate course than it was to achieve a 'perfect' grade for the missed assignments. Once she'd planned out what was possible and was confident that her acceptance onto her postgraduate course was still very possible, she was able to work through and complete the outstanding work.

Now that you know how important the right mindset is to achieve your goals, take positive steps each day to improve your mindset. When you catch yourself talking about how busy you are, or how you don't have time, try to reframe it into a more positive light.

In the next chapter, we'll be looking at how to track your time to identify where your time is currently being used and how to improve.

Chapter Four – Easy Time Tracking & Analysis

"Waste your money, and you're only out of money, but waste your time, and you've lost a part of your life."
Michael LeBoeuf

The first step to taking control of your time is to identify what you are actually doing with the time you have now. You'll be surprised at how much you can achieve in a day when you take a cold, hard look at where your time is currently going and apply proven techniques to get more done in less time.

If you're not a fan of tracking your time, then bear with it. The end results will be worth it, we promise. Understanding how you currently use your time will help you understand which time management techniques will have the biggest impact on you.

It might be tempting to try to skip this part, in favor of making a list of what you know you do, and how long it takes. Unfortunately, that simply doesn't work.

If someone asked you to describe what you did with your time, you'd probably have a pretty good idea of which tasks you do the most. It might surprise you to learn, however, that we tend to underestimate or overestimate exactly how long we spend on certain tasks.

Think of how time passes when you're doing something you love. Perhaps watching your favorite movie or spending time with friends. Hours can pass with you barely noticing the time.

Now think of how time passes when you do something you don't enjoy, or something difficult–like holding a plank for a minute. Those 60 seconds will feel much longer than 60 seconds of pleasant chat with a friend.

This phenomenon of time seeming to move faster or slower for different tasks can lead us to miscalculate exactly how long we spend on each activity if we're not actively tracking it. There's also the hidden psychological effects of society's expectations and our current emotions.

For example, working Moms often overestimate the time they spend on household chores, and underestimate how much sleep they get. This is partly because society's perception is that working Moms are overworked and always tired. There's a chance that they will feel that saying they get enough sleep or don't spend hours a day on chores will somehow make them look like a 'bad' Mom who isn't doing enough.

It's also partly because they do feel tired. The mental stamina needed to run a household with kids and hold down a full-time job is high. Not many people enjoy chores, so it feels like you do spend a lot of time on them. If you're also feeling wiped out at the end of the day, your perception will naturally be that you don't get enough sleep. Without tracking it, that perception persists even if you do actually get enough sleep.

Sociologists have discovered that when we take part in surveys about how we spend our time, we're prone to overestimate the time we spend on some tasks, like housework, by as much as 100%.

Then there are the activities we forget that we've done.

Have you ever had that panic as you've gotten halfway to work that you didn't lock the door, or turn the stove off, only to rush back and discover that you did, you just don't remember it?

When we repeat certain actions regularly, they become less memorable. While we certainly don't expect you to track your time so thoroughly as to note locking your door or turning off your stove; some tasks that we repeat throughout the day for short bursts can actually add up to a big chunk of time over a week. If you forget to track them, then chances are you won't remember doing them.

By tracking your time, you'll give yourself an accurate baseline from which to improve, plus the data to see where you might be able to win back time easily.

Here's an example of where tracking time helped a work-from-home dad spend more quality time with his kids.

Real Life Case Study: Chris

Chris recently left his corporate job to work as a freelance writer and look after his twin daughters, aged five. His wife is a partner in a law firm, and they wanted to have more flexible childcare arrangements without relying on a nanny. The girls attend kindergarten on weekdays, and so Chris would have some time to pursue his freelance career.

Chris loves working from home and looking after the girls, but his initial plan for working from home was flawed. When he estimated how much work he could get done while they were at kindergarten, he grossly underestimated how long most tasks would take him. He factored in time for research, but he underestimated how long that work would take. He also overestimated how many words he was able to write per hour, and assumed he'd be able to take on and complete more work per week than the reality.

Some mornings, after dropping the kids off at kindergarten, Chris struggled to get into the swing of researching and writing. He often finds his flow just before he needs to leave to pick them up. Once the girls were home, Chris wanted to have time to play and do activities with them. He began to feel guilty for resorting to placing them in front of the TV with a snack most days while he caught up with work.

Chris decided to keep track of his time, and his word counts in a journal. He combined this with an online activity tracker that would log which websites and apps he spent the most time in.

When he looked back at the data he'd collected, he realized that some of the time he was logging as 'research' was being taken up with other tasks. The online activity tracker showed that during this time he would swing between research and various other activities, including social media and handling household bills and admin online.
He also noticed that he would jump between research and writing, usually until the mid-afternoon. As he came across something relevant, he would open his document and start to write until he needed to check something, and would then move back to research. Analysis of his log also showed that once he had been writing continuously for around 30 minutes, he found his 'flow' and his writing sped up dramatically.

Chris decided to make a small change to the way that he worked. Instead of mixing the research and the writing, he would spend the first ninety minutes after dropping off the kids doing research only and making detailed notes. After a short lunch break, he would spend two hours writing, without using the internet to do any additional research.

He would simply leave a placeholder in the document if he needed to check something. He would then have a further thirty minutes to either take care of household bills, check social media, or do a little more research before leaving to pick up the girls.

With the same amount of hours available and the same amount of work, Chris managed to almost double his output. He removed the need to continue working after the girls came home from kindergarten, and was able to spend more quality time with them before his partner came home from work.

How to Easily Track your Time

Track your time as closely as you can for one week, including outside of office hours. The most important thing is that you are as accurate and consistent as possible when you are tracking your time. Remember, the only person who will be looking at these is you. You'll need an accurate picture of what you currently do so that you can implement the right strategies and see the best results.

Be as specific as you can about how you're spending your time, but don't make it more time consuming than it needs to be. Logging 15 minutes as on social media, is fine, but putting 10 minutes Facebook, 5 minutes Twitter, etc. will help you pinpoint more precisely where your time is going. In the same manner, try to note exactly what kind of work-related tasks you are completing: emails, meetings, phone calls, report writing, etc; and when you are interrupted or distracted.

When it comes to how you physically measure your time, you can use:
- a journal
- a spreadsheet
- an online tracking system
- a combination of all three

Try to keep it as simple as you can and use whatever feels most natural to you. Your method of tracking time should feel as unobtrusive as possible.

There are numerous online time tracking systems. These include services that will log which websites you use and how long you spend on them as well as project management tools. Many tools even allow you to create task lists and use a timer to track how long you spend on each individual task.

Some people find the more automated tools like these easy to use, whereas other find them unnecessarily complicated or forget to switch them on and use them. If you use your phone a lot, there are mobile apps that can measure how long you spend on social media and other time drains. Often people will check social media numerous times throughout the day, almost as a reflex. Some smartphones even do this automatically as part of their operating systems now. If you don't use an app to track this, note down as soon as possible on your time tracker each time you are using social media on your phone.

A journal or a simple spreadsheet is the easiest ways to keep track of your time. If you are using a journal or spreadsheet, divide each day into 30-minute blocks, and mark down what tasks you are doing in any 30-minute period. Using 30-minute time blocks makes it simple to track what you are doing. If you become used to tracking in 30-minute blocks, you could potentially try 15-minute blocks. Tracking shorter time blocks will give you an even more thorough breakdown of where your time is going. Anything less than 15-minute blocks is unnecessary.

Make it your mission for the week to log your time regularly and accurately. If you think you will forget to track your time, set a reminder or alarm for every 30 minutes.

Analyzing the Results
You've collected your data, now you need to analyze it to see where you can claim back some time, and where your personal pinch points are. A lot of the time, simply reviewing the time log is enough for you to be able to see where you could make immediate, positive change. These are 'quick wins' where you can gain some time back straight away.

A deeper analysis can help you see less obvious patterns where your time isn't being used as effectively as it could be. These are the areas where you may want to put in extra work to build new habits or develop better time management strategies.

To begin your analysis, go through and categorize the activities. Separate them out into high-level categories and add up how much time you spent on each category:

- Work
- Socializing
- Sleep
- Entertainment (social media, television)
- Family time

- Eating/drinking
- Exercise
- Household chores and errands
- Other activities

You may not need to use all of these categories, depending on your own lifestyle. Create sub-categories where needed; for example, you may want to break down 'work' into tasks relevant to your role such as emails, phone calls, meetings, report writing.

When you look at your time log, see what stands out the most. If you were successful in tracking your time accurately, you will probably see that you spend a large chunk of time on non-essential activities. Are there any obvious areas where you spend time on things that are not important? Is there an excessive amount of TV, or are you spending time outside the office answering emails that would wait until you were in the office?

If you can identify clear areas where you can change your habits to gain additional productive time, make a note of them and resolve to use that time more effectively. For example, you may want to get fit but only spend only an hour a week exercising. If you spend ten hours a week watching TV, you can take some of the TV time and devote it to exercise instead to move you towards your goal.

One category that should be protected is your sleep time. Everybody's sleep needs are a little different, but it's prudent to aim for at least 7 hours of sleep a night.

Getting enough sleep is crucial to productivity, so don't be tempted to try to gain additional time by reducing your sleeping hours. If your tracker shows you aren't getting enough sleep, your top priority should be to remove non-essential activities to make enough time for sleep above anything else.

When you've identified the 'quick wins' to gain back a little time, take a deeper look at what you're doing during your productive time:

- How much of the time that you were 'busy' was spent on tasks that moved you towards your goals?
- How much time was spent on tasks that did not need to be done, or were less important than other outstanding tasks?
- How often were you interrupted by emails, phone calls, or colleagues calling by your desk?
- How much of the work you did could be easily delegated?

Pay attention to how productive you are at certain times. Do you get the most done early in the morning, or later in the afternoon? Could you schedule the biggest, most important tasks to coincide with your peak productivity?

Look for trends on the days when you felt you achieved the most. Are there common themes such as fewer interruptions, location, and how you feel about the task you are doing? Can you use those themes to your advantage?

If you see that you are regularly interrupted through the day, or are switching tasks frequently then try to take steps to reduce this. For example, set certain times that you will be available for calls and other interruptions and do your best to stick to those times. If particular people are causing most of your interruptions, then try to manage their expectations about when you will be available.

Your goals and any important and urgent tasks that cannot be delegated should be your main priority. Most of your productive activities should be moving you closer to achieving your goals. That's the real secret of successful people. It's not luck; it's ruthless prioritization.

Real Life Case Study: Joanne

Joanne is an office manager for a busy accountancy practice. Part of her role is managing admin tasks for the practice's three senior partners. Keeping on top of her workload requires her to be very organized, and for the most part, she balances her workload very effectively.

A change in tax legislation and the addition of a new senior partner has recently made that balance much more difficult to maintain. Each partner is assigning her urgent projects relating to the change in the legislation, and she is often interrupted in the middle of one task to complete something urgent or provide an update for one of the partners.

The systems she had in place previously to manage her workload and keep her organized couldn't cope with the additional strain. Joanne decided to keep track of her time for one week using a simple spreadsheet. She broke down her time into 30-minute sections and took just one minute out of each 30-minute block to log what she was doing, and for who.

The next Monday morning Joanne sat down to look at what the time log was showing her. She was astonished at how often she was switching between different tasks, either at one of the partner's request or under her own steam.

While she couldn't change the amount of work she had to do, she could change the way she handled that work. She set daily and weekly goals for each partner's projects and made sure that she finished the required task on one before she moved on to work on another.

Joanne built in 'buffer' time of an hour a day to field urgent requests. She also became much more confident at managing the expectations of each partner and challenging 'urgent' requests to identify if they were truly urgent and allowing her to prioritize better.

Just this simple change to the way she was working allowed her to gain back control of her time. While it didn't reduce the tasks or the workload, having time to focus entirely on one task at a time allowed her to finish each task faster and feel less stressed.

The fact is that you can't control time. It carries on, regardless of what you do with it. It's what, and how you prioritize that will make the most difference.

We'll investigate prioritization much more closely in Chapter Six, but in a nutshell, time is a commodity, and it is finite. There's nothing you can do to increase the hours you have in the day, but what you can control is how you use those hours. Good time management isn't about getting things done faster; it's about doing more of the right things.

Now you know how much, or how little time you are spending on what is important, it will become easier to cut back on activities that don't move you forward towards your goals. Yet, without the right kind of goals, your time management will still be ineffective. In the next chapter, we'll be looking at how to set the right goals so that you can manage your time most effectively.

Chapter Five – Increased Productivity and Better Time Management

"People with goals succeed because they know where they're going."
Earl Nightingale

Before we get into some practical ways to manage your time, let's take some time to think about your goals. Goals are at the root of all effective time management; they give you both long-term vision and short-term motivation. When you know what you're aiming towards, you know where to devote the most of your time.

Having clear goals also helps you accomplish more of the things you care about. When you are clear about what you are aiming towards, it becomes easier to reach it. What would you like to have more time to accomplish?

If you don't already have clear and defined goals, take some time now to think about what you want to achieve. This is the time to daydream and identify everything you want. Don't get caught up with how you will achieve it, or even if it is achievable. Think as big as you can and imagine what you want your life to look like.

These goals can be both work and life-related. You might want to achieve a promotion, take a distance learning course, live in a foreign country, or write a book. Whatever it is you want to achieve, write it down. Make them goals you can be passionate about, and not simply what you think might be expected of you to achieve.

This doesn't mean that a small amount of common sense

doesn't apply. Someone with no medical education can't become a brain surgeon in 2 years, for example. But almost all big dreams can be achieved when you're sensible about the timeline. Want to write a best-selling novel? Or become a CEO? You can do those things, no matter what your current circumstances.

Make sure your goals are really goals and not tasks. Your goals aren't the things you write down on your to-do list every day, those are your tasks. They're definitely related – or at least, they should be, but they are different. Your tasks are the actions you take to move you towards your goal. They're the journey – the goal is the destination.

A 'goal' of exercising for six hours a week isn't really a goal – it's a task. The goal is to improve your health and fitness. The six hours of exercise a week will move you towards that goal at a good speed, but those six hours aren't really the destination – they're the journey. 'Writing a book' is also a task dressed up as a goal. Your actual goal is probably not the actual writing of the book – it's to become a published author.

When you have a clear idea of what your goals are, think about how much of your time is currently spent on tasks that move you towards those goals. Ideally, most of your time should be spent on activities and tasks that get you closer to your goals.

Is that the case for you? Or are you spending most of your time on mundane tasks like picking your laundry up from the dry-cleaner, or doing the grocery shopping?
Of course, you can't practically avoid having any tasks on your to-do list that aren't moving you towards a goal – but your aim should be to have most of your tasks do so. Mundane tasks like picking your laundry up from the dry-

cleaner, or doing the grocery shopping are inevitable tasks but rarely link to one of your goals.

Ideally, you will have plenty of goals; some large, big-picture goals and other, smaller goals. There should also be a mix of long-term goals and short-term ones.

Once you know your BIG goals, the ones that define the life you want, then look at smaller, supporting goals. These are more short-term. What do you want to achieve in the next 12 months? The next month, the next week? Ideally achieving these goals will contribute in some way to your big picture goals.

Having a clear picture of your short and long-term goals is important for many reasons:
- So that you know where you're headed
- So that you know what success looks like
- So that you can break down your goals into manageable tasks.

Let's take 'writing a book,' which we noted earlier is more of a task than a goal. Some people might argue that writing the book really is the goal in itself. And if you literally just want to own a manuscript that you wrote, then it could be the goal. But that's unlikely. If you're going to write a book, then you probably want people to read it. In which case, you'll want to have it published.

Leaving the goal as 'write a book' means you have to change your goal when the book is written, now you have to publish it. Not having the whole goal identified means that you may not have included steps to get it published in your tasks or smaller goals.

Having it all tied into a bigger goal keeps you motivated as you're reminding yourself of your real desire and not just focusing on the hard work it takes to get there. You're reminding yourself why you're putting in the hard work.

Seeing the outcome you want motivates you to do the actions. Writing down the actions alone just looks like hard work, and even though you know what the outcome is really, you will be less likely to follow through with the tasks.

Think about Your Why
To set goals that motivate you and drive you to achieve them, you need to know why you want them. If you want to be a famous singer, why is that? Fame? Fortune? Love of music?

Be real with yourself here. Many musicians will tell interviewers that their 'why' is the love of music and wanting to inspire and enrich other peoples lives via their music. It's possibly absolutely true, but your why doesn't have to be noble or an interview worthy answer. It just has to matter to you. Only you need to truly understand your 'why' because you need to understand what is driving you.

If you want to be a famous singer because you love singing, and you want to be famous to show childhood bullies you're not a loser, that's fine. If it's because your teacher at school told you it was stupid, and you want to prove them wrong, also fine. As long as it's really important to you, your why doesn't matter to anyone but you. However, you do need to understand it so that you can be sure it's the right goal.

Sometimes when we sit down and think about the 'why' of a goal, we don't have a compelling reason. "Become a successful investment banker," is a suitable goal but if the 'why' is simply because they make a lot of money, then it's not the most compelling reason. Many occupations can make you a lot of money, so why not choose one that you would also really enjoy?

If you want to be an investment banker because you want to make a lot of money, your heart sings with joy when you look at numbers on a spreadsheet, and you read the stock market like Mozart reads music, then go for it! That's definitely a compelling reason why!

The other issue is that the real goal is rarely the money itself. There's nothing wrong with wanting to make lots of money but if your goal is to be earning a lot of money, then there's probably another 'why' underneath that. Maybe your real 'why' is that you want to earn a lot of money to support a lifestyle where you can travel. Maybe it's to own a large house in a nice area. Or maybe you want to be able to financially support other family members.

Get really, really clear on your 'why'. It's what will sustain you through the inevitable hard moments of achieving the goals you've set out for yourself.

Write your Goals Down
Now that you know what your goals are, write them down. Writing them down makes them more real and makes you more likely to achieve them. If you want to increase your chances of success even further, visualize them as you write them down and repeat those visualizations regularly.

Writing your goals down also allows you to focus on them. Now that they are written down, you will be able to easily identify whether what you are spending your time on is helping you to achieve them.

Although there are several studies showing that people who write down their goals are more likely to achieve them, opinions on why writing down your goals works are divided. Some attribute it to the law of attraction and sending a clear intent to the universe.

The law of attraction might be something you don't set much stock in, but many successful people are big believers. Jim Carrey famously wrote himself a cheque for $10 million in 1990, when he was flat broke. He dated it for November 1995. By the time the date on the cheque arrived, he'd just agreed a $10 million contract for Dumb and Dumber.

Others believe that writing things down simply helps cement them in your mind, and helps you clarify the goals, thereby making them easier to achieve. It's also possible that writing them down forces you to be a little more specific and clear on what your goals are, something I'll cover that in more detail shortly

In the long run, it doesn't really matter why it works. The fact that most people who do achieve large success have written down their goals at some point should be enough to spur you on to do the same.

Choosing what to Focus On
You've written down your list of big goals, and now you need to pick some of them to work on. Choose three big goals from your list to start work on now.

Why three goals? It's a manageable number to work with, without fracturing your focus too much. If a lot of your goals are interlinked and support each other, you may be able to focus on more. I'll still refer to it as your three goals throughout the book, however, as it's a manageable number for most people.

Don't worry that your other goals will be ignored, longer term as you accomplish a goal, you can go back and add in another goal from the list. While the end game is to achieve all your goals, trying to focus on too many at a time can make it overwhelming and set you up for failure. Laser focus on a few at a time will help you when you're managing your time.

So how do you choose the ones you focus on right now? This is a little personal, and you should follow your gut but here's a couple of methods to help you narrow it down if you're struggling:

Option One
Choose one goal that is so big it's scary, and the idea of achieving it makes you more excited than any of the others.

Choose another goal that won't take a very long time to achieve, so that you can build a little momentum and experience success.

Choose a final goal that in some way supports your really big, scary goal. This just makes achieving the big goal a little easier. For example, if your big scary goal is to leave the corporate world and become your own boss, and another goal is to learn how to build websites, the two things conceivably interlink.

Option Two
Another method is to look at the balance of the goals across different areas of your life.

Depending on what you have written down, choose one career specific goal, one personal development/education goal, and one lifestyle (spiritual, relationship, health) goal.

Write your three goals down at the beginning of every day, or at the top of every to-do list, or keep them somewhere prominent to remind yourself often what you are working towards. Keeping your goals at the forefront of your mind makes you more open to opportunities that present themselves. Have you ever noticed that, for instance, when looking for a new place to live that you start seeing rental/for sale signs everywhere? You may have thought it was just a coincidence but it's not! Making sure you have somewhere nice and safe to live is something that is important to you and your brain will immediately recognize this. It will log this in your subconscious and whenever there is an opportunity presented (such as a rental sign), it will magically help you to see the related opportunity.

Don't be afraid to change your goals if you want to. At different stages of our lives, what's important to us can change, and what seemed like an important goal five years ago might now seem less relevant or desirable. That's ok, you're allowed to change them. Just try to avoid changing them because you think they're unachievable. Almost nothing is unachievable, having goals that truly tap into your desires is one of the most powerful motivators you can have to achieve the things you want.

Now you know what to focus on, you'll want to break it down into smaller tasks so that it becomes actionable and less daunting.

Identify any key steps that you will need to take to reach

the end goal, and document these in the SMART format. We'll cover this in a moment if you haven't worked with SMART goals before. If we go back to our example of becoming a bestselling author within 5 years we might break it down like this:

- Write a chapter by chapter outline of the novel within the next two months
- Write the first draft of the novel within the next six months
- Edit the first draft within three months of completion
- Contact a minimum of twenty literary agents within two months after editing

There will be more steps than this on the way to the main goal of becoming a bestselling author, but these are the immediate tasks you could begin to tackle. You can break these down even further and set smaller, daily or weekly goals which would be the tasks on your actual to-do list.

Make your goals SMART

Now you have your 'big picture' goals, and you've identified what you want to work on immediately, you'll want to convert them to SMART goals: Specific Measurable, Achievable, Realistic, and Timed.

Specific: You need clear and specific goals so that you know exactly what you're aiming to achieve. So 'write a bestselling book' is good, but 'write a crime thriller that reaches the NYT bestseller list' is better.

The best goals are specific about how they will be achieved, including any resources and materials that you might need to succeed.

Measurable: You need to make your goal measurable so that you know when it has been achieved and you can measure how close you are to achieving it if you haven't gotten there yet.

With goals that have a number attached, it's straightforward. Goals that are specifically financial are usually easy to measure. 'Achieve the no.1 ranking in Google for the search term 'biscuits' would be strange, but a measurable goal. Once you hit the no.1 spot on Google, you've achieved your goal.

Let's go back to a previous example: become a no.1 best-selling author. Looks measurable on the surface, until you dig deeper and it becomes a little less clear-cut. What counts as a bestseller? Which ranking system do you want to use? There are multiple categories and subcategories on Amazon. If your book hits the top of one of their category charts you get a no.1 bestseller flag on your book while it remains at the top of the category. Yet your no.1 bestseller in one category could be a sub 10,000 ranking in the overall Amazon bookstore.

To know how best to measure this goal, we'd have to return to the why. If you want to be a bestseller because you want to gain authority with readers in your genre, getting to the top of your category may be enough. If you're looking for international fame, then you might want to reframe your goal to say 'become a New York Times bestselling author' or any other book ranking chart that best fits your own 'why'.

If your goal is less obviously quantifiable, then you'll need a different way to measure it. Many things can have a number attached to them but beware of attaching a number simply for the sake of it. If your goal is to become healthier by next year, you might choose to frame it as 'lose 10 pounds by Jan 1st.'

If you're not already overweight that might be the easiest way to make it quantifiable, but the not the best option for your circumstances. Instead, you might choose to do a fitness test now and identify the amount of improvement you want to see when you repeat the test on Jan 1st.

There are many ways to make things measurable but resist the urge to just slap a number on your goal. Tap back into your 'why' to ensure you're measuring it in the most effective way.

Achievable: Your goal needs to be something you can attain, but don't be afraid of stretching yourself and dreaming big. Try to keep your view of your own ability out of the assessment of what's achievable and just apply common sense.

A goal of 'Learning Mandarin in two days' is going to be unachievable. 'Learning Mandarin in twelve months' would be potentially challenging, but not completely ridiculous. Dream big, but don't deliberately set yourself up for failure.

Relevant: You should make sure your goals are relevant. How do they tie in with your big vision for your life? Do they support your other goals, or at the very least not contradict them?

Sometimes the 'R' in SMART is also listed as 'Realistic,' but as that's pretty much covered under 'achievable,' we're using the 'relevant' tag for our purposes.

Timed: This links closely with 'Measurable,' but you should make sure that you have a timeframe on your goals. Giving a clear timeline means that you're more likely to achieve it.
It also helps you to identify if you're taking too much on. If you've set 3 really big goals to be achieved in the next 3 months, you might want to reconsider the timeline on one or two of them.

By assigning an achievable timeframe to your goals, you can achieve anything you want to.

Many of these aspects of SMART goals are closely linked. Often, making a goal specific automatically makes it measurable, and a clear timeline can mean that it will also tick the 'achievable' box. Once you've written a few goals in the SMART format, you'll find that it becomes second nature to frame your goals this way, and you won't need to keep referring back to the framework.

Real Life Case Study: Judith

Judith felt like she never had time, ending each day tired and never getting anywhere. She would fill her to-do-list every single day. Most days she managed to get through the whole list but was missing a sense of purpose and lasting achievement. She didn't dislike her job as a legal secretary, but it no longer challenged her.

Judith was always productive, in that she got lots of tasks done every single day. Her colleagues were often in awe of how much work Judith could handle. While she wasn't immune to a little occasional procrastination or a free afternoon in front of the TV, she wasn't spending a lot of her time idle.

It wasn't until she sat down and wrote down her goals, that she realized she was constantly putting goal-related tasks to the bottom of the list. She was treating them as activities to be squeezed in and not as something to be prioritized. For example, she'd spent the last 5 years saying she was going to look for a new job, and yet had still not updated her CV. Something else always seemed more important.

It seemed so obvious, but now with her goals written down it was harder to ignore them. Judith decided to tackle her career goals first. She made time to update her CV and refresh her professional qualifications to make her a more attractive prospect. Within six months she had a new job and was moving on to achieve some of her other goals.

Judith was still always busy, but now she could see how those tasks were small stepping stones to larger successes, and not just an endless list of things to do. Each evening she would reflect on her achievements that day and feel a sense of satisfaction and achievement, knowing why she was completing the tasks on her to-do-list.

Time will slip by if you allow it to. If you don't really know how you want to spend it, it will be almost impossible to spend it wisely. Even if you take great care to not waste it, without goals you may be constantly busy but never really achieving anything of importance.

Now that you've finished this chapter, you should have all your goals clear in your mind, and a plan for which goals will be your focus in the short-term. In Chapter Six, we'll look at how to fit in all of the mundane but essential tasks alongside your goal tasks using effective prioritizing.

Chapter Six – Prioritization – It's Easier Than You Think!

"The key is not to prioritize what's on your schedule, but to schedule your priorities."
Stephen Covey

We've covered the fundamentals of time management and have identified what your goals are and therefore what you should be spending your time on. It's time to move on to how to look at how to prioritize all those tasks on your to-do list. It's important to make sure that your activities are moving you towards those goals as well as taking care of all the mundane chores and errands.

In this chapter, we'll cover a few different systems for prioritizing work. All of these have been used successfully to help people take control of their time, and the systems work well when used together. Make sure that you are implementing at least one of these systems to prioritize your activities. It doesn't matter which one, they all work well, what is most important is that you are implementing something that works for you.

The Eisenhower Matrix

Dwight D. Eisenhower was considered to be one of the masters of time management, and the first prioritization system we'll look at is commonly known as the Eisenhower Matrix. The matrix got its name from the fact that Eisenhower believed that people would benefit from identifying how urgent and important their tasks are. He was even said to use this system himself to prioritize tasks.

To quote the man himself: *'What is important is seldom urgent, and what is urgent is seldom important.'*

The matrix was popularized by Steven Covey and features in his book *'The 7 Habits of Highly Effective People'*. It is made up of a square, divided into four quadrants.

You assign each task to a quadrant based on the task's urgency and importance. "Important" relates to the impact of not doing the task. "Urgent" relates to how quickly it needs to be done.

Important tasks are rarely urgent, and vice versa. Clearly identifying how urgent and important a task is will help you to prioritize and make better decisions.

The Eisenhower Matrix quadrants are:
1. Top Left: important and urgent
These are tasks that need to be done immediately, or at least in the next 24-48 hours, and not doing them would have a significant impact. Often these are 'crisis' tasks, like handling a broken boiler in the winter, or responding to a serious customer or client complaint.

Look at whether better organization would have removed the need to complete this task, or reduced the urgency, such as regular boiler maintenance!

You can't completely avoid all crisis tasks, so the best way to accommodate them is to leave a little 'wiggle' room in your schedule. This way you can reschedule other tasks to handle them if they do arise.

2. Top Right: important but not urgent
These are tasks that move you closer to achieving your life

goals. They are tasks that you know in advance need to be done, and they should be scheduled in but often aren't.

They're also the tasks we often procrastinate on, or we place more 'urgent' tasks above them, constantly knocking them down the priority list. Unfortunately, they're also the ones most likely to propel us towards our goals and make our lives better if we completed them. Yet they rarely have a set-in-stone deadline, and so we continue to react to the more time-sensitive tasks because it seems like the right thing to do.

3. Bottom Left: urgent but not important
These are the tasks we normally fill our days with, and they're usually a blend of planned and reactionary tasks. Answering emails, some chores, handling interruptions and last-minute work requests from other people.

None of it is important, in the sense that if it didn't get done nothing life altering would happen. However, there is usually a sense of urgency attached to the task. Often, the urgency is based on other people's priorities rather than your own.

Limiting these can be difficult, and while they're rarely important, they do need to be done. We'll take a look in a short while at some tactics for reducing the amount of these tasks, and ways to reduce the amount of time they take.

4. Bottom Right: not urgent or important
These are the tasks that we should spend the least amount of time on and are the tasks that can be removed to make way for more important activities.

They're often dismissed as 'time wasting' but relaxation activities like reading fiction and watching television are part of this quadrant. While these activities should be limited, they do have a part to play in your overall wellbeing.

Internet surfing, social media, and those addictive YouTube videos of animals being hilarious also live in this quadrant. Those activities still can have a place in a balanced life, but the trick is to ensure that these tasks are not eating into time that would be better used on something else

Using the Matrix
It's easy to see how this matrix relates to entrepreneurs, executives, and any traditional work tasks. But how is the matrix helpful for non-work activities and stay at home parents?

Here's an example of the matrix in use for a single mom: Anna is a single mom of three boys, with a part-time job during school hours as a receptionist for a dental surgery. Her main career goal is to become a virtual assistant so that she can work from home. Her days are filled with multiple tasks, and to keep on top of things Anna keeps a to-do list in a notebook in her purse.

Her to-do list is her lifeline, and she's diligent about putting every task on there so that it can't be forgotten. A typical day's list includes things like grocery shopping, taking the boys to soccer practice and playdates, restocking the dental surgery's stationery supplies, and taking the car to the car wash.

The tasks seem never-ending, and Anna tries to finish them all each day, but sometimes struggles to complete it. While her list is comprehensive, it's not in any particular order, and her mindset is simply to get it all done, without applying any real priorities to it.

Anna had seen the Eisenhower Matrix before, but considered it to be something that managers and executives used, and unnecessary for the kind of tasks she completed. But she was beginning to feel frazzled keeping up with her list and had to try something to help.

One Thursday evening, she separated her notebook page into the four quadrants and wrote the Friday's list onto the matrix.

In quadrant 1: urgent and important, she wrote down that she needed to pack the boy's bags to spend the weekend with their dad, as she hadn't managed to find time earlier in the week. She also needed to restock the dental surgery's stationery supplies, as she'd noticed they had run out of compliments slips and pens yesterday.

In quadrant 2: important but not urgent, she wrote down that she needed to organize the dental surgeries client database, to make her job a little easier when booking in appointments. She also wanted to book a virtual assistant course, to move closer to her dream of working from home.

In quadrant 3: urgent but not important, she wrote down that she needed to get the boys' hair cut, take out the trash, clean out the refrigerator, go grocery shopping, prep meals for next week, and organize the boy's closets.

In quadrant 4: neither urgent nor important, she wrote down that she'd like to read the novel currently gathering dust on her nightstand, to watch the movie she'd recorded on the DVR, and go on a lunch date with an old friend.

Anna realized that she spent most of her time on items in

quadrant 3, and also that the activities in quadrant one could have been avoided by being more proactive. The items in quadrant 4 were the tasks she liked the most, and she was likely to skip tasks in quadrant 2 in favor of those.

If she spent more time on quadrant 2 tasks, she could avoid some of the quadrant 1 tasks happening at all. A more organized database would make it easier and faster to find patient information. This would mean she'd have had more time at work to check stationary supplies and order before it became a crisis issue. Moving towards her goal of working from home in the future by booking a course would mean she'd spend less time commuting and have more time to pack the boy's bags.

Seeing how much of her time was spent on quadrant 3 really opened her eyes to the fact that she needed to somehow remove or reduce those tasks where possible.

Eliminate, Automate, and Delegate

Now that you've applied the Eisenhower matrix to your tasks, it's time to identify ways to remove and reduce some of the non-important tasks from your list. To do this, we'll look at eliminating, automating, and delegating tasks.

Eliminate

Take a look at your quadrant 4 tasks that are neither urgent nor important, are they really necessary? Could they be removed completely? Be strict and realistic about this, but don't leave yourself with no relaxation time at all!

Now, look at your quadrant 3 tasks that are urgent, but not important. Are there any that could actually be removed? Don't be afraid to start saying 'no' to people if you find that most of your non-important tasks are generated or handed to you by other people.

Sometimes the idea of saying no can be scary. But it doesn't mean you have to be rude, or upset people. You might be surprised at how often and readily people will accept you politely refusing to take on additional, potentially unnecessary tasks.

Some of the kind of tasks you might say no to are:
- Picking up a colleague's overflow work when you already have more than enough to do.
- Taking on extra tasks in the office when someone else's skills and availability make them a better fit.
- PTA volunteer work, when you have other more important work that needs to be done.

When you say no, you don't have to be rude, but equally, you don't have to over-explain yourself. You have a right to say no. If saying no doesn't come naturally, you're not alone. Women tend to be even more susceptible to this than men, as they can sometimes feel like it's their role to keep people happy.

To take the stress out of saying no, think of the kind of people, tasks, and situations that it makes sense for you to say no to. Once you have a list, prepare how you will say no in advance. This way, you'll be less likely to panic about how to decline, and accidentally end up saying yes anyway!

Sometimes, a flat-out no might not be possible, but the level of urgency the person requesting is allocating to the task could be out of sync with your own priorities. In these situations, you may not be able to say to no to the task, but it could be perfectly possible to renegotiate the deadline. You might even limit the scope of the task to reduce the impact it will have on your own time management. You can also suggest delegating all, or some of the task to somebody else more suited, or with more available time.

Automate

How many of the tasks in quadrant 3 that must be done are repetitive tasks that you do daily, weekly or monthly? It's possible you'll be able to automate some of these repetitive tasks and free up your time and focus for other things.

We'll cover automation tools and their uses in Chapter 10, but for now, let's look at a few tasks that would be perfect for automating:

These could be tasks like:
- **Client invoicing**. If you invoice the same amount each month, set up recurring invoices. There are several tools online to do this, and many of them are free to use.

- **Automatic payments for household bills.**

- **Social Media posting.** If you're managing social media accounts for your business then consider scheduling this if you don't already. Again, there are lots of free options for this that will allow you to schedule content in advance and free up some of your time.

- **Emails.** Do you send the same information over and over again in your emails? Most email clients have the ability to store canned responses. This way, the information you need will populate at the click of a button and save you typing it out over and over. Many smartphones also have a keyboard text replacement shortcut that allows you to quickly input words and sentences that you use often. For example, a common one is to have 'em' followed by a space to auto-populate your email address. This can save you both time and potential errors when you're replying to emails and messages on the go.

- **Subscription services** for household and grocery items you buy regularly.

Delegate
So you've taken out all the unnecessary tasks, and identified tasks that could be automated. What's left? Can it be delegated?

Some people struggle with delegation for various reasons. They may feel guilty for 'offloading' work or worry that it won't be done to the standard they would do it. Perfectionists often struggle with delegating tasks.

How to delegate effectively:
- Delegate tasks that are within that person's skill set.
- Provide clear instructions to prevent miscommunications.
- Delegate responsibility for the task and allow them to get on with it–don't check up every two minutes on them, as it's counter-productive. If the task requires it, follow up at an appropriate, pre-agreed time.

Delegation isn't uncommon in an office setting, but it's also possible to do at home. Getting your children to help with age-appropriate household chores can both lift some weight from you and teach children essential life skills at the same time.

Outsourcing
If you don't have co-workers or other people in your life to delegate tasks to with the right skills, then outsourcing could be the answer.

You can outsource almost any task, from hiring a cleaner

for your home to getting yourself a virtual assistant to manage your emails or your social media. There are people with the right skills willing to do most tasks for a fee.

When deciding if a job is worth outsourcing, consider the cost of paying someone to do it and compare that with the value of what you can realistically achieve with the time you gain back. If paying a cleaner allows you to take on an additional client at a higher rate per hour than you are paying the cleaner then it is worth it. If it allows you time to go to the gym and build a healthy body, it may also be worth it in a different way.

It's also important when outsourcing to be sure that the person you hire has the right skills for the job. People often want to hire the cheapest person for the job, but balancing competence with your budget is the safest way to do it. Especially if you're outsourcing business tasks or trusting someone to care for your children.

If you're outsourcing business tasks, you can look for particular qualifications, or you can pay them to do a small 'test' job to start with and take it from there. Finding the right person to help you with your workload can be a huge blessing, so make sure you get it right first time.

The 80/20 Rule (The Pareto Principle)

The 80/20 rule is a simple but effective principle that originated in economics but can be applied to practically any area of your life. Discovered by the Italian economist, Alfredo Pareto, the original principle was that only a small portion of any group is really significant, approximately 20%.

In time management the Pareto Principle suggests that 20% of your tasks are supplying 80% of your results, and moving you towards your goals. Your aim is to identify what that 20% is and eliminate, automate or delegate the remaining 80%, or as much of it as possible.

Once you know what those 20% tasks are, you need to make sure that they are scheduled in your planner or calendar with a date for completion. Resist the urge to de-prioritize these tasks once you know what they are. These are the tasks that deserve your attention the most, as they are the ones that will have the most impact on your results.

If you've done the Eisenhower Matrix exercises, take a look at the matrix with your current tasks. Are roughly 20% of your tasks in the top right quadrant important, but not urgent? This is often where these tasks that are driving results reside.

Decision Making

So far in this book, you've been making a lot of decisions. You've made big decisions about what your life goals are, and what to focus your time on. You've also made smaller decisions like which tasks can be removed completely from your to-do list and who you can delegate tasks to.

In that time, you've probably also made thousands of other decisions. What to wear, which mug to pour your coffee into, which route to take to work. Our days are made up of thousands of decisions–as many as 35,000 each day by some estimates.

Barack Obama famously always wore either a gray or a blue suit. He consciously chose to do this, to remove an unnecessary decision each morning on what to wear. It sounds ridiculous, but decision fatigue is a real thing and the strain of making too many decisions can impact how effective you are at making sound judgments when they really matter.

Every time you make a decision you are weighing various options against each other and applying different sets of information and criteria. Even something as small as choosing what sandwich to eat for lunch is using up mental energy.

You can counteract decision fatigue by making as many decisions in advance as you can. Get your outfit ready to wear to work the evening before and prepare your lunch to take with you. If you prefer to always drink the same coffee brand, you know what to pick up at the grocery store and don't spend time or mental energy deciding.

Real Life Case Study: Julia

Julia is a busy working mom. As a project manager, she makes multiple decisions at the office every day. Making the wrong decisions could delay the project or cost the company hundreds of thousands of dollars to put right.

At home, she's constantly making decisions for and about her family. From choosing the children's and her own clothes each morning to cooking meals that everyone will eat and that provide them all with the right nutrition. Some days after a long day at work making decisions, her decisions on what to cook for her family aren't as nutritious as she'd like them to be.

Julia wanted to reduce her mental load and cut the risk of

decision fatigue at work while also saving time and improving her family's health. When she looked at where her time was going, she identified that getting herself and everybody dressed each morning and preparing meals was taking up most of her time at home.

She decided to get organized. She rearranged the closets and drawers so that instead of having tops in one drawer, blouses in another, they were organized in outfits suitable for various occasions and different weather. This way, each morning she would easily be able to lay her hands on a complete outfit instead of trying to choose coordinating items.

She planned out her meals in advance for the month, which had the added benefit of making grocery shopping faster and cheaper, as she was also reducing accidental food waste. Each item she purchased would be used in her planned meals, and each planned meal would be a healthy, balanced meal.

Planning ahead also allowed her to only consider once what each family member liked to eat. Julia could make sure that everybody could have their favorite healthy meal once a week. She could even cook in large batches and freeze leftovers to save even more time the week after.

The time investment to get organized like this was initially high. But once her systems were in place, keeping to them saved her hours each week. It also reduced the number of decisions she was making at home so that she could save her mental energy to deal more effectively with project decisions at work.

Using the tools and techniques in this chapter will help you to prioritize much more effectively, make better decisions and identify which tasks are worthy of your time and effort.

Getting organized and applying these tools and principles can help you see faster results in reaching your goals. However, it's always important to make sure that you are balancing your time to maximize both your results and your personal health and wellbeing. We'll take a look in Chapter Seven at how vital it is to make room for adequate sleep and self-care.

Chapter 7 – Realistic Self-Care

"The time to relax is when you don't have time for it."
Sydney J. Harris

It's easy to put self-care, sleep and relaxation activities on the back burner, and to grab fast food while we rush from one task to the other. But the busier we are, the more we need to take care of our bodies to avoid stress and eventual burnout.

Some of the physical effects of stress are headaches, insomnia, digestive issues, and irritability. These can make it harder to stay productive when we're tired, irritable and feeling unwell. Overworked, stressed people make more mistakes and take longer to complete tasks. If you're burning the candle at both ends, you'll eventually run out of reserves, and then nothing is going to get done at all!

The best way to avoid stress is to look after your physical and mental health properly. Consider it an investment in your own well-being, and essential to your time management efforts. We've discussed prioritizing, now it's time to investigate why you should be your number one priority

How To Get Better Quality Sleep

Most of us know how vital sleep is for our wellbeing, but we don't consistently practice great sleep habits. Numerous studies have shown that your productivity takes a hit when you don't get enough sleep.

The difference in your mental state and productivity after a good night's sleep is drastic, but we don't always get the amount of sleep we'd like. Parents of young children, in particular, often complain of not getting enough. Yet we don't often prioritize sleep in the way that we should. Even though we don't prioritize it, we often do want more. When we wake up in the morning, we wish we could cling to sleep just a while more. Yet in the evenings the lure of a late-night movie, or reading just one more chapter, can keep us burning the midnight oil more often than we should.

Sometimes we find ourselves working late into the evening to catch up. It can work as a one-off solution for a busy day. But if you find that you regularly work long into the night, then you should do whatever you can to reclaim that sleep time.

Even just one hour of lost sleep can impact your energy, mood and stress levels the following day, and if we keep skipping sleep these issues only get worse. Sleep debt accumulates, and scientists have discovered that simply having a lie-in on weekends isn't enough to make up for sleep lost throughout the week.

If you're not getting enough sleep, you'll potentially make more mistakes, be less able to concentrate, and less capable of remaining calm under stress. You're basically a lot less efficient, which spells disaster for your time management efforts!

So, if you're guilty of skipping sleep, it's time to recognize how important it is to your overall health and wellbeing to get enough shut-eye. However, you're certainly not alone. It's estimated that a huge 40% of Americans don't get the recommended 7-9 hours of sleep per night.

The Different Stages of Sleep

Not all sleep is equal, and your sleep is broken down into cycles. You go through 4 different stages of sleep in every 90-minute sleep cycle. It's the final, Rapid Eye Movement stage of sleep that has the most benefit to you in terms of feeling rested and restored. If you don't get enough REM sleep, you'll feel the effects the next day.

The first 3 stages of sleep vary from light sleep all the way through to very deep sleep. These stages are all similar in that our eyes do not move beneath our closed lids. These 3 stages are grouped together as Non-Rapid Eye Movement sleep–or NREM. While REM is usually considered the most beneficial stage, these NREM stages are also important for healing and repair states.

REM sleep is where our eyes do move beneath our closed lids. They don't move constantly during this phase, but they do move quite regularly. It's often linked to a state of dreaming.

While each sleep cycle is roughly 90 minutes long, the amount of time spent in each of the 4 phases of sleep varies through each cycle. In the first cycle of sleep, REM is normally around ten minutes long and increases over each cycle until the last few cycles, where it can last up to an hour.

Interestingly, the amount of REM you get isn't just related to the number of hours you sleep. Studies have shown that regardless of the time you fall asleep, people will enter the REM phase of sleep for longer periods over the later hours of the night. These longer periods of REM can continue all the way up to 7am! We also tend to spend less time overall in REM the more we age.

How Much Sleep is Enough?
Ideally, you should be aiming for 7-9 hours per night, although our sleep requirements do change throughout our lives. Some elderly people only need 6 hours of sleep or less, and babies will need to sleep a lot more than 9 hours a day.

The exact amount of sleep you need varies but aiming for a 7-hour minimum is a great start. It's also important to try to get good quality sleep. Here are some tips to help you maximize your sleep time:

Go to bed at the same time every evening. While this may not be possible every single day, you should make a concerted effort to go to bed at the same time each night. Choose a time that will allow you to get at least 7 hours of sleep and then make it a habit to be in bed at this time.

Limit your device time in the evenings. The kind of light that tablets, smartphones and your television emit is blue light. Blue light can disrupt your natural sleep rhythm and prevent you from dropping off to sleep at a normal time. Ideally, shut off these devices a couple of hours before bed, and do something else. You could read either a printed book or an e-reader that uses an e-ink screen instead of backlit LED. You could also make this dedicated self-care time where you meditate or do some light yoga and stretching. Try to avoid strenuous exercise before bed as it can make you more awake and alert.

You could even make this part of a bedtime 'ritual' to signal to your brain that it will soon be time for sleep. If you've implemented the first tip and set a specific time for going to sleep, take it one step further by creating a bedtime ritual. Ideally, you would include relaxing, soothing activities to help you wind down.

Cut out caffeine after lunchtime. You should be avoiding caffeine for 8-12 hours before bedtime. While it might feel like the effects of a cup of joe wear off after a couple of hours, it takes over eight hours to leave your body. So, switch to decaf, or even better–water or herbal tea–after lunch. Drinking caffeine too late in the day can disrupt your sleep and mean that the sleep you do get is lower quality than it should be.

Try to avoid alcohol. Sometimes it's tempting to have a nightcap to 'help you sleep,' and it will often help you drift off faster. However, it's a false sleep economy. Alcohol blocks your REM phase of sleep, so while you will technically be asleep, you're not getting the full benefit of each sleep cycle.

Keep your bedroom for sleep. Your bedroom should be a haven of rest. By using it to watch TV, work, or play on your smartphone, you're training your brain to think of it as a multi-use space. By keeping it strictly for sleep, it will automatically become a place where your mind starts to prepare for sleep when you enter. Make sure your bedroom is a comfortable temperature, and that your mattress and pillows are in good condition to promote a good night's sleep.

To Snooze, or not to Snooze?
One of the worst things we do, and most of us do it, is hitting the snooze button in the morning. Because of the way the sleep cycles work, your alarm is probably going off during a deep phase of sleep. This means you feel tired and groggy when the alarm wakes you. So, you feel like

having just another ten minutes will really help you be refreshed ready to start the day–wrong!

You've started the cycle all over again, and the effects of that can last for hours.

When your alarm goes off, get up. If you have the luxury of not having to get up at a specific time, then try to allow yourself to sleep until you wake naturally. Within reason, of course! Waking naturally at the end of a full sleep cycle will mean that when you do get up your brain is ready to start the day.

If you don't have the luxury of a fully flexible schedule, investing in a special alarm clock that wakes you with slowly increasing light that mimics sunrise can help. There are also apps you can get for your smartphone that monitor movement while you sleep. They will wake you at an appropriate time in your sleep cycle to prevent any adverse effects. Most of these apps require sensors that are only available on some newer smartphone models.

There are also safety considerations to take account of if you are going to sleep with your phone on the bed–we don't want any fire hazards!

Naps
If you have the opportunity, napping during the day has been shown to boost productivity, focus creativity and overall energy levels. Keep that sleep cycle in mind if you choose to nap. 15-20 minutes will be refreshing but setting the alarm for 50 minutes could rudely awaken you from a stage 3 deep sleep and leave you groggier than you were before!

If you have the time, a full 90-minute cycle can have extra

beneficial effects, including aiding learning retention. If you're unable to find time to nap, or you work in an office environment, you can simply make even more effort to have a restful night's sleep every evening.

Meditation – It's Not What You Think!

Meditation has been growing in popularity for the last two decades. It's no longer just a new-age practice, it's something that regular people are beginning to incorporate into their daily lives. The benefits of meditation are well documented, and they include:

Stress reduction
Almost everyone knows that regular meditation can help you keep your stress levels in check. It can even decrease blood pressure and helps you sleep better. If that's not a good enough reason to try meditation, then I don't know what is!

Improved focus and concentration
Daily meditation improves the connection between parts of your brain that are related to focus. Research from the *University of Sheffield* showed that mindfulness encourages persistence with tasks and allows for a more sustained period of focus than people who don't meditate.

Less procrastination
Regular meditation can reduce your tendency to give up on tasks by promoting self-acceptance and promoting self-motivation. According to a study by the *University of Windsor*, procrastination is driven by negative thoughts and feelings of unworthiness. Meditation reduces your tendency to be overly self-critical and therefore reduces your propensity to procrastinate.

Reduces the effects of aging on the brain
People who meditate regularly retain more cognitive function, especially memory function, than people who don't meditate.

But isn't meditation just one more thing that takes up your valuable time? Of course, you'll need to plan meditation into your day, but just ten minutes a day can actually boost your overall time management massively.

In much the same way that employing an accountant pays for itself in tax savings, daily meditation will pay for itself with improvements in sleep, focus, and reduced procrastination. In fact, the real question isn't can you afford to make time for meditation? It's can you afford not to?!

Meditation covers a wide variety of practices, and they all have very similar benefits so you can choose the method that works best for you. Here are a few basic types to get you started:

<u>Just sit still</u>
This is often referred to as mindfulness meditation. Don't worry about how long you do this for when you first start. It sounds ridiculously simple, but it can actually be very hard to just sit and not do anything when you're used to rushing around all the time. The caveat here is that you need to be completely device free, and ideally alone with your own thoughts. Simply sit down, get comfortable and take a few slow, deep breaths.

Think about how your body is moving while you inhale and exhale.

Then just allow your mind to go where it wants to, without trying to react. Thoughts will come into your mind, they always do, but you simply decide that they don't matter at the moment. If ignoring the thoughts makes you too anxious, you can keep a pen and paper handy to note down anything you want to explore later. But for now, once they are written down just let them go.

Guided Meditation
If you feel like you need assistance, or instructions to know you're doing it right (perfectionists, we're looking at you!) then a guided meditation might be just what you need.

There are many mediation apps available for smartphones, all of which have several programs of guided meditation. Most of the highly rated apps require a subscription to access the majority of the meditations. However, you can usually try the basic relaxation meditations for free before you decide if these are your best option.

You can also find guided meditations online for free with a quick search, or purchase them on CD. If you choose this option, make sure that the device you are using to play the guided meditation on doesn't become a distraction.

Chanting Meditation
You might feel a little silly initially, especially if you don't live alone! But chanting meditations offer a fast way to slip into a relaxed state. These kinds of meditations involve sitting comfortably, cross-legged on the floor and repeating a sound or mantra to clear the mind. A popular one is the 'Om' sound.

While chanting you focus on the sound of the mantra, and you can transition whenever you like into silent meditation. Simply allow yourself to do whatever works for you at the time

Breathing exercise for stress reduction
Most meditation focuses on breathing for a good reason. Most people breathe in short, shallow breaths, but just a

few minutes of deep breathing can help reduce stress and tension. If you're feeling a bit of a mid-afternoon slump, deep breathing will also help re-energize your body and stop you turning to caffeine.

This exercise can be done anywhere. Even in a meeting (unless you're the speaker!).
Start by getting comfortable. You can lie down, or simply sit in a chair with your back straight and feet on the floor. Now take a deep breath in through your nose, and instead of only drawing the breath into your chest, draw it all the way down into your belly. You should see your belly rise as you breathe in. Breathe out slowly through your nose.

Repeat this at least four times, and up to ten times to feel the benefit of lowered anxiety and stress, and increased energy.

Exercise
A little like meditation, exercise is one of those things that you might feel like you don't have time for. Perhaps you have bad memories of high school gym class, and you don't want to make time for it. But like meditation and sleep, it's an activity that will repay the time investment a hundredfold if you commit to it.

Exercise will improve your energy levels, increase your productivity and improve your sleep quality.

It's also a great stress reliever, allowing you to forget your worries for a short while. It doesn't even have to be a huge time investment, even twenty minutes each day can make a huge difference if you were previously sedentary. If you can stretch it to half an hour, or even an hour–even better.

Two of the most common barriers a lot of us put in place to

exercise are:
1. I can't afford a gym membership. You don't need to join a gym to get a good workout. You don't even need specific equipment. If you have some previous experience with exercise, there are videos on YouTube from qualified professionals that you can do at home, for free. If you haven't exercised for a long time, it's a good idea to attend classes or see a personal trainer for a few sessions until you are comfortable that you understand proper form.

If that isn't possible, you can always take up jogging, go for long walks with friends or alone, or join a local sports team. Check with your doctor before taking up anything particularly strenuous, but most people would benefit greatly from adding in a little exercise to their daily lives.

2. I don't have time. We've covered this in other chapters, but of course, you do have time to do anything you want. It's just a question of priorities. You can even break down your twenty or thirty minutes of activity into 2-3 very short sessions across the day if it's easier to fit it in that way. In fact, short sessions of High-Intensity Interval Training have been shown to be very effective for improving fitness and shedding extra weight.

A lot of people enjoy exercising in the morning, as they feel it gives them extra energy and motivation for the day. This increases their productivity and more than makes up for the time spent exercising. Consider what you could cut out of your morning routine, or even delegate, to fit in some exercise instead.

Real Life Case Study: Steven

Steven is a busy account manager. His daily routine used to

consist of snoozing his alarm several times before finally getting out of bed at 6:45am and pouring a cup of coffee. After his coffee, he would be ready to shower, dress and leave for work.

When he arrived at work for 8am, he would have another cup of coffee and chat with some colleagues before he attempted to start his day. When he did finally begin, he would start with basic tasks that required little concentration. Around 10am he would be awake, alert; ready to make some phone calls and start his most important tasks. He often used to joke that he wasn't functional before at least three cups of coffee.

When he got a promotion and some bigger clients to handle, he began to struggle to keep up with his workload. One of his friends suggested that he incorporate exercise into his morning so that he could regain a couple of productive hours in the mornings. Steven was reluctant at first. He wasn't overweight or very unfit, and he didn't feel like he had time to exercise. He also couldn't see how exercising would gain him more time.

His friend convinced him to give it a try for just one month. Steven's new routine consisted of getting up as soon as the alarm went off at 6:30am, drinking a large glass of water and then going for a fifteen-minute jog instead of his morning coffee time. The first couple of mornings he didn't want to do it, but he pushed through anyway.

By the beginning of the second week, he was almost looking forward to getting up and going for a run. The fifteen minutes he spent jogging was great to clear his mind, and by the time he arrived at work, he was ready to get straight to it. In fact, he could start on important tasks with no 'warm up.' His first cup of coffee was now at 8am when he arrived at work, but he no longer needed to drink the coffee to be ready to start making client calls.

He found he was more alert all through the day, and better able to solve problems without becoming stressed. He was also beginning to sleep more deeply at night, making getting up each morning easier. He felt healthier, more relaxed, and was able to get through his workload much easier. By the end of the month, he was convinced enough to make exercise a lifelong habit.

There are so many benefits to exercise that it makes no sense to leave it out of your priorities. It reduces stress, reduces the risk of numerous diseases, and increases blood flow to the brain - and therefore mental performance. Plus, the feel-good endorphins boost your mood making you more positive and able to tackle challenging mental tasks.

If exercise isn't already part of your daily routine, it can be hard to build the habit. Initially, there will be some days when you think you can't fit it in. But putting in the time and effort to make it a habit will pay off in the long run. Do what you can to make non-exercise days the exception to the rule.

Nutrition Tips

Nutrition is also often overlooked in typical time management discussions, but how you feel is crucial to how productive and motivated you are. And what you eat makes all the difference to how you feel.

We often think of diet in terms of our weight and appearance, but what you **fuel** your body with can make a huge difference to your energy levels and overall

wellbeing. And as we've seen in this chapter so far; the better you feel, the more productive you are.
Eating a poor diet full of processed foods, caffeine and alcohol can lead to low energy and 'slumps' in energy through the day; fatigue; feeling sluggish; higher levels of stress; as well as health-related illnesses like diabetes and high cholesterol.

Eating an optimum diet benefits you across many areas of your life, but exactly what is optimum will vary by person. The details of creating an absolutely optimum diet for health and productivity could fill a whole new book, so while we'll cover just the bare minimum of it here, the three key basics are:
- Drink more water and less caffeine or alcohol
- Avoid as much processed food as you can
- Eat mindfully and stop eating when you are full

Simply following these basic rules should lead to an increase in energy and productivity as well as longer-term boosts to your health and wellbeing. Of course, any improvements are dependent on what your diet was like to begin with!

Going beyond those three basic rules, here's what you need to know about eating for health and productivity:

Eat lots of vegetables in a wide variety of colors. Fresh, frozen and canned all count. Vegetables are packed full of vitamins, minerals, and fiber that help keep your energy levels stable and your body running as it should.

Eat 1-2 pieces of fruit a day. Fruit is nutritious and contains lots of vitamins and minerals like vegetables, but unlike vegetables, fruit can contain a lot of sugar. It's still infinitely better than eating candy or drinking cola but avoid eating very large quantities of fruit on a regular basis.

Eat healthy proteins at each meal. Eggs, fish, lean meats and tofu or beans can all provide you with a good amount of protein.

Eat unrefined carbs as they digest slower, contain more fiber and vitamins, and won't give you that post-lunch slump. Oats, whole-wheat bread, brown rice, quinoa and sweet potato are all great choices.

Have 2 portions of dairy each day. Yogurt is a great choice and is often easier to digest for most of us than other dairy sources. A small piece of cheese per day can also fit in nicely with a healthy diet and provides calcium alongside other vitamins and minerals.

Don't be scared of fats! We need a certain amount of fat to keep us healthy, and it's very important for proper brain function. The problems begin when we eat a diet high in fried foods or trans-fats found in lots of processed foods. Healthy fats like the ones found in avocado, olive oil, and oily fish are essential for a healthy body. Even some saturated fats like grass-fed butter are needed in small amounts for optimal health.

Cook from scratch. Processed foods often contain all manner of additional ingredients. Sometimes these are for added shelf-life, and sometimes they are for taste. Processed versions of foods often contain way more salt and sugar than you would use cooking the same food at home.
Obviously, you don't need to take it too far. Baking your own bread is a great way to make sure it's as healthy as possible, but it may not always be practical. Just check the ingredients labels and keep the food you buy as close to its

natural state as possible and your energy levels should soon rise.

Supplements
It can be tempting to take supplements as an easy alternative to eating a wide variety of fresh food, but your body is designed to get its nutrients from real food. When you eat a balanced diet of natural, unprocessed food, your body gets the right nutrients in the right amounts to function properly.

Lots of nutrients work synergistically, so taking too much of one nutrient in supplement form can throw the others out of balance. For example, taking too much zinc in supplement form can sometimes cause a copper deficiency.

Only people with a specific medical reason should need to take supplements. For example, an anemic may need an iron supplement. If you are considering taking any supplements other than a basic multivitamin, speak to your doctor first.

Hydration
Drink more water–This is advice repeated everywhere. Woman's magazines tout it as the cure-all for skin concerns, and it's credited with everything from clear skin to increased athletic performance and better sleep. Good hydration is essential to most of your body's functions.

When you drink enough water, you'll notice that you have more energy, sleep better and may even shed a pound or two of excess weight!

As with everything, balance is key. Drinking too much

water can be bad for you–but how much is too much? The common advice to drink 8 glasses of water a day is unlikely to have any adverse effects at all, and you can drink much more than that without any issues if your kidneys are in good health.

Your body can process roughly 27-34oz of water each hour, but exact amounts will depend on your bodyweight. Your body can only process that much water per hour in extreme heat or during very heavy exercise, and you shouldn't be aiming to drink that much water.

For optimal hydration, aim for one 8oz glass of water as soon as you wake up, and then another 8oz glass every two hours sipped slowly to keep your body working at optimal levels. This way, you stay well hydrated all day and should see all the benefits of your water consumption.

Spreading out your water consumption across the day helps to keep your internal functions running smoothly. Trying to drink your daily 'target' of water by gulping down an 8oz glass three times in an hour means you don't get the full benefit of being hydrated. Your body simply flushes out what it doesn't need at that time. Drinking your 64oz by the early afternoon and then stopping could still leave you dehydrated by the evening.

A simple way to test if you are hydrated enough is to pay attention to the color of your urine. If it's a pale yellow, then you're hydrated. A dark golden color or a strong smell can indicate that you need to drink more water.

<u>Caffeine and Alcohol</u>
It's not enough to just drink more water. You will also want to reduce caffeine intake if you want to increase your productivity. If you're crying inside at the thought of

drinking less coffee, then don't despair. You can still drink 1-2 cups a day, and if you're a heavy coffee drinker, don't cut it out immediately.

Instead, cut down by 1 cup every week until you are drinking no more than 2 cups per day to avoid headaches and other unpleasant withdrawal symptoms. The time at which you get your caffeine fix can also impact your productivity. To make sure you get enough sleep, drink your last cup of coffee before noon.

Ideally, you would also keep your alcohol consumption as low as possible, but if you are enjoying an alcoholic drink or two, try to alternate with a glass of water for each alcoholic drink you consume. That way you'll stay better hydrated, and your energy levels will be less impacted the next day. As we covered earlier in the chapter, alcohol can impact your sleep quality as well as dehydrate you, so you should still avoid it when you can.

Sugary drinks including fruit juice should also be avoided as they can give you a brief energy spike followed by a crash later on. Anything high in sugar will have this effect, so watch out for all sugary drinks and mixers as they can easily sabotage your healthy eating efforts as well as productivity.

Now that you know how important it is to build healthy habits don't delay implementing them! Many people will read this chapter and have the best intentions of 'starting on Monday' or 'starting after the big party' or some other reason to not start right now.

Often, it's the most important steps that we put off and procrastinate on, taking in favor of other things. In the next chapter, we'll look a little deeper at the problem of procrastinating and how to avoid it.

Chapter 8 – Ending Procrastination Forever!

"Procrastination makes easy things hard, hard things harder."
Mason Cooley

Do you find yourself procrastinating more often than you should?

If so, you're one of many. Procrastination is a common problem, and there are many reasons people procrastinate. It's often mistaken for pure laziness, but the real reasons we procrastinate can be surprising and complex. In this chapter, we'll investigate why you might be delaying taking action, and what to do to tackle the problem.

We'll also look at tips and tricks to help you overcome procrastination and move you closer to achieving your goals.

Why do we Procrastinate?
There are lots of reasons why we procrastinate, and many different ways we do so. Sometimes, even the least house-proud of students will become more interested in cleaning their room than writing an essay. Others might put off writing the essay in favor of more fun tasks like watching movies or posting on social media.

Procrastination is normal, but procrastinating too often, and on the wrong things, can be detrimental to your health, relationships, and your career.

So why do we do it?

Understanding what causes you to procrastinate is the first step to beating it. Here are some of the most common reasons people procrastinate.

Fear
Fear is one of the things our lizard brain understands. The lizard brain can find fear in the strangest places. It's afraid of failure, and it's afraid of success. How often have you put off going to the doctor–not because you're too busy, but because you're worried they'll give you bad news? It's a surprisingly common problem. People put off seeing a medical professional in case they are seriously ill. Common sense tells us that getting fast treatment is the best course of action. But our lizard brain doesn't want us to have to deal with the problem, so it helps us bury our head in the sand. Our lizard brain justifies our reticence for us, labeling it merely as 'being busy.'

You might be afraid of failure. People often procrastinate when they feel unconfident in their abilities. They know the task must be done, but they just can't face the idea of doing it poorly. Unfortunately, leaving it until the last minute can mean that you rush the task, and do complete it badly. It becomes a self-fulfilling prophecy and keeps you in a place of self-doubt.

You might be afraid of success. Being more successful than your partner, or your friends can be a scary thought. You're comfortable in your relationships, and while you want success, achieving your goals might make others view you differently.

If you're feeling the fear, the best way to combat that is to just do it! If you're afraid of failure, remember that not doing something is the biggest failure there is. If you do it and it's not perfect, then you'll have learned something–but chances are it will be just fine.

If you're afraid of success, looking over your goals and your personal 'why' should give you the kick of motivation you need to push through.

Give lizard brain the finger and take action!

Lacking Clarity
This one is common for students and professionals who often have tasks delegated to them. If you aren't sure what or how you're supposed to do something, you might be tempted to put it off until later.

Perhaps you're embarrassed to ask your teacher or boss to clarify the instructions. Maybe you think they will believe that you weren't listening when the instruction was given, or that you are stupid.

Maybe you think researching will help you understand–but you haven't done the research yet. Why not? Because you're scared that you won't find the answers you need, and you don't want to deal with that and go back to the source for clarity.

Lacking clarity can also cause you to lack focus, which causes procrastination. Before you know it you're two hours from a deadline, and it's impossible to meet. If only you'd asked for clarity earlier!

If you lack clarity on a task, then do something about it. Most people will welcome questions about a task they've set you. Asking questions shows that you are interested and invested in doing the task to the best standard you can.

Don't be afraid that it will make you look bad - it's much

more likely to show you in a good light!

Lacking Motivation
Perhaps you just don't want to do it. You might not see how this task benefits you, or you might not have set yourself goals. Without goals, you might struggle to find motivation as you can't tie it to something you're aiming for.

When you spend too much time doing tasks that you can't see the benefit of, your motivation will drain away until there's none left at all. Figure out what the benefit of doing the task is to you and aim to tie it to one of your goals. If you can't, consider delegating or outsourcing the job.

If you can't delegate or outsource the task, and it's something that you have to do yourself, then get it done as soon as you can. Perhaps even offer yourself a reward for completing the task. Maybe a coffee break, or your favorite lunch.

Another good tactic to motivate yourself if you can't see the benefit to doing something is to consider the risk if you don't do it. Avoiding negative consequences can be as powerful a motivator as the anticipation of a reward.

Lacking Energy
If you've not been following the best practice in the previous chapter, and aren't getting enough sleep or eating well, you might find that you seriously lack energy.

Persistent fatigue that doesn't respond to the advice in the previous chapter should be investigated by a doctor. However, a few lifestyle changes and applying proper time management techniques can help you deal with any general tiredness and lethargy you might be feeling.

If you feel like you constantly lack the energy to get anything done, make an effort to take better care of yourself. Your energy levels should soon return to normal. If they don't, consider seeing your doctor to rule out any medical conditions.

Perfectionism

We've covered this in Chapter 2, but it bears repeating. The need to do a task perfectly can stop you from doing anything at all. If you're putting something off because you're worried you won't do it well enough, then it's time to put that fear to bed. Just do it because good is good enough.

Don't let perfectionism become your excuse to delay taking action. The end result is likely to be that you do a less than perfect job anyway because you ran out of time.

Aiming to do the best job you can is admirable but remember that requires you to allow yourself enough time to do the job and to factor enough time for probable procrastination.

Overcoming Procrastination From Today!

So now you know what might be driving your procrastination, but how do you overcome it?

If you've identified the root cause of your procrastination, you're halfway there. But if you're a serial procrastinator who regularly struggles to get stuff done, some more general techniques might work for you to take back control.

Break Tasks Down into Smaller Pieces

If you're avoiding a job because it seems too large, break the job down into manageable steps. If you're clearing out a room in your house, perhaps divide it into quadrants and aim to clear a quadrant at a time. If you're writing an essay, break the task down into stages. For example, creating an outline, doing the research and taking notes, writing the first draft, editing and fact-checking and a final proofread. Do one stage at a time, and it won't seem so daunting.

If you're not sure how to break the job down into clear steps, then identify the first action you can take to progress it and do that. This works well for big goals like 'Become an investment banker.' If there's an exam to be taken, but you haven't even cracked open a book, your next action could be to spend two hours studying the first module.

Once you take decisive action, the momentum carries you through. You'll complete a small task, and you're suddenly ready to do the next small task, and before you know it, the whole thing will be completed.

Use your Planner

Put your tasks in your planner, diary or calendar. Somewhere you will see them, and it will be obvious when you haven't done them. Moving tasks from a vague 'to be done' list and scheduling a concrete time and date makes you more likely to do them.

It's human nature to not want to 'fail' once you've committed to something, so putting it into your calendar means that not doing it is a failure.

You can also use your planner to schedule rewards right after completing the tasks but if you don't do the task, you don't get the reward.

The 2-minute Rule
If there's a task that takes 2 minutes or fewer, you have no excuse. Just do it. Immediately. Getting rid of smaller tasks cluttering up your to-do list can immediately relieve stress and alleviate the feeling that you have too much to do and not enough time.

There's also the risk that if you leave those little tasks, you'll forget to do them at all. Because they're so small, you can easily justify saying that you'll do it later, but then never get around to it.

So, make that phone call, pay that bill online, cancel that subscription, or whatever you have noted down to do later that's a 2-minute task. You'll feel better and reduce the risk of completely forgetting about the task because it's so small! It's also great because it gets the 'doing' ball rolling. Completing even the little things gives you a sense of accomplishment and makes you feel more positive about tackling and completing the bigger tasks you may have.

Shrink the Task
If you're putting something off, then try starting the task by doing a tiny amount of work on it. This is similar to breaking a big task down into smaller tasks but works

better on tasks that don't lend themselves well to clear 'steps.'

So, set yourself the goal of writing two sentences, or ironing one shirt, or completing one section of the report, or just spending ten minutes on a task. Often, you'll find that once you've done that bite-size part of the task, you'll be happy to carry on and do more. Starting a task is always the hardest part. You might even finish the whole task in one sitting.

Accountability Partners

Another great trick for making yourself less prone to procrastination is to get an accountability partner. An accountability partner is a co-worker, friend or family member that you 'team up' with to keep each other accountable.

You share the tasks you have to get done for that day, week or month with your accountability partner. Agree on regular check-in intervals with each other to assess your progress. Knowing somebody will be asking about your progress can keep you motivated. Nobody wants to have to admit that they haven't accomplished something they committed to.

Accountability partners work great when people are doing similar tasks to you. In those circumstances, they really appeal to the more competitive among us. So, if someone else you know is working towards a similar goal, or has a similar task list then consider pairing up and watch both of your productivity levels skyrocket!

Good Procrastination

We tend to label all procrastination as bad. If you're putting something off, you're procrastinating, and that's bad. But sometimes, procrastination is necessary. You may realize that you don't have all the information or tools to complete a task. In which case, it needs to be pushed back until you have what you need to complete it properly.

In fact, sometimes 'precrastination', where you complete tasks immediately even though they don't have to be done now can be worse. Replying instantly to an email instead of thinking the response through, for example.

If you act quickly, under too much pressure, you might end up with the wrong outcome. This is where planning is key. Rearranging your priorities is not procrastinating, in fact, it's an essential time management skill. Don't be afraid to adjust your plans; sometimes priorities and responsibilities shift and you need to react accordingly.

When we refer to procrastination in this chapter, we're referring to the tasks you're putting off for no good reason.

If you really are pushed for time, make sure you use the Eisenhower Matrix to identify what can be postponed. Postpone low-importance, low-reward tasks that aren't supporting your key goals.

Avoid postponing tasks that contribute to your long-term goals. When they're long-term goals, it's easy to push them back indefinitely to deal with more time-sensitive tasks. However, as we discussed in Chapter 6, it's almost always a bad idea.

Procrastination and Discipline
In the end, beating procrastination is about discipline. The discipline to accept when you're procrastinating, to identify

why and then to do something about it.

It's the doing something about it that's the hardest part. It takes determination and hard work to push through the issues behind your procrastination. The good news is that determination is a habit you can learn, it's not a mysterious personal quality that some people have and others lack.

So, how exactly do you build determination and blast through procrastination? In the best-selling book *'Eat That Frog'*, Brian Tracy advised that you should commit to doing the worst tasks first. As Brian explains:

"Mark Twain once said that if the first thing you do each morning is to eat a live frog, you can go through the day with the satisfaction of knowing that that is probably the worst thing that is going to happen to you all day long."

Now, nobody is suggesting you actually eat a frog! The frog represents the worst task on your list. The task that you know is your biggest procrastination risk. You're scared of it, you find it boring, or it's just something you're not looking forward to.

When there's a task on your list you don't want to do it can cause you to procrastinate. The problem is compounded when it's the most important or urgent task. Not only do you not do that particular task, you don't do the other tasks on the list. You put the other tasks off because by starting those you're acknowledging that you're ignoring the first one. So you somehow find other things to do and don't tackle your list.

It's a lose-lose situation.

The best way to deal with it is to acknowledge what you're

doing and the fact that you're avoiding it; then get it done. Break it down into tiny steps if you have to but get started on that task, or 'eat that frog' straight away.

When you blast through those tough tasks early on, first-thing, the rest of your day is easier, more productive. Some days, you might have several frogs. Brian Tracy's advice here is to eat the biggest, ugliest frog first and then move on to the next.

With determination and practice, blasting through your worst tasks first will become a habit. And once you see the results it can bring, those frogs will start to look tasty!

Real Life Case Study: Dave

Dave is an experienced accountant, running a successful accountancy practice.

He would spend a lot of his time explaining to his clients how important it was to take the time to file receipts and expenses and to be prepared for the tax deadline. Yet every year, Dave would find himself procrastinating, on none less than his own tax return!

He knew what to do, how to do it, and in theory, it wasn't even a big task. Yet he just couldn't bring himself to sit down, focus, and fill in the forms. He'd happily process them for his clients but his own was still left untouched until deadline day every year.

While it did always get done in the end, the stress of having it constantly in the back of his mind took its toll on his overall productivity and well-being. He would put off smaller tasks, thinking that he couldn't justify doing them if he hadn't yet filed his tax return. But he still didn't take action to get it done.

When he took the time to think about why he was putting it off, Dave realized that it was because it didn't obviously contribute to any of his big goals. Yet the benefits of getting it done and the risks of failing to do it, were significant. On this occasion, the fear of the consequences was much more motivating than any reward.

When he decided to *'eat that frog'* and not allow himself to get anything else done until he'd filed his tax return, he suddenly found tax season a much less stressful experience.

He was able to give his clients his full and undivided attention as he wasn't constantly stressing over his own tax return, and he could relax and enjoy time with friends and family without the nagging guilt of his unfinished paperwork.

The frog, in this case, was really more of a tadpole but it was still causing a big problem for Dave. Once he got disciplined and identified why he was putting it off, he was able to take positive action and kick procrastination to the curb.

While this chapter covers lots of practical tips and tricks to help you overcome procrastination, ultimately, it's up to you to act and to stop putting things off.

Discipline is a key factor, but there's another part to the procrastination and productivity puzzle and that's focus. Without focus, you'll struggle to complete even the simplest of tasks. In the next chapter, we'll look at ways to sharpen your focus and turn yourself into a productivity machine.

Chapter 9 – How To *Actually* Get and Keep Focus

"It's better to do one thing at a time and give your full concentration."
Erica Fernandes

In a world where we're connected 24/7 it can be difficult to maintain focus and concentration on one task. If you're used to multitasking and bouncing between tasks, the idea of sitting down and tackling your work in one sitting might feel daunting. In this chapter, we'll look at ways to enhance your focus and remove the distractions that leave us with half finished tasks at the end of a day.

The Key To Deep Focus

In Chapter 2, we discussed why multitasking is a false friend of good time management. As a quick recap, some multi-tasking is necessary in life, just ask the parents of small children. For them, without multitasking, nothing would ever get done. You might also hold a conversation with a friend while you both run on a treadmill at the gym, or you might listen to music as you cook dinner.

Where multitasking gets murky, however, is when we try to multitask regularly with important tasks and believe it will help us to be more efficient. The fact is that multitasking doesn't really exist.

What you're really just doing is **switching** between tasks. And unless one of those tasks is an ingrained habit or something that can be done on autopilot, like listening to music or walking on a treadmill, then switching between tasks simply doesn't work. For example, the act of listening to the music isn't taxing your brain in any way, so you can focus on cooking without ruining the food.

Most of us have experienced multitasking, and while it can seem like we're getting more done, often that's not really the case. Think of the last piece of work you did that you were proud of. It might have a been a great essay, a presentation that won you new clients, or a thorough closet clear out. The chances are that for a reasonable period, you were focused on only that task.

Think about that feeling you get when you're completely in the zone, focused on the task at hand, and you don't look at the clock even once. That level of focus is exactly where you need to be when you're working on important tasks. The big tasks, the ones that move you closer to your goals. Your goals and your future deserve your full focus.

In order to make strides towards our big goals, deep focus is a necessity.

Harness your Natural Energy Flow
Think back to Chapter 4 where you tracked your time. As part of that exercise, you looked at whether there was a pattern to your most productive times. Do you get the most work done in the morning or the evening? Is the post-lunch slump a reality for you, or do you power through tasks after your midday meal?

There's lots of advice floating around about making the most of your productive times. You'll often see it said that most successful people are up at 5am, as you will get more done early in the morning. For a large number of people who follow that advice, it will work well. But if you're one of those people who find that a 5am start leaves you less productive overall, rest assured there's nothing wrong with you–And you're not doomed to mediocrity either!

We all have our natural peaks and troughs through the day. The key to harnessing your natural energy is to understand and work with that energy. In order to do this properly, it's imperative that you are following the advice in Chapter 7. You should be getting enough sleep, eating a healthy diet and taking time for relaxation.

If you're not taking care of your body, your energy levels are naturally going to be out of sync. In short, that's not your natural energy flow; it's how your body responds under stress. If you're getting adequate sleep and nutrition and not working yourself into the ground, pay attention to when you are most productive, most creative and most energetic.

By using this natural rhythm to your advantage, you can give a real boost to your time management practice.

Importance of Flow and How to Trigger it

If you have a big, important task to work on, then ideally, you'll want to achieve a state of flow. Flow is that state we discussed earlier where you're in the zone. For writers, it's when the words literally flow from your mind through your fingers and onto the page. When you're reading it's that point where you're totally immersed in the fictional world you're reading about or are absorbing the information on the page rapidly.

When you're in a state of flow, the world around you is tuned out. You're not wondering what to have for dinner, and your brain isn't going to interrupt with a reminder that you didn't answer Aunt Margaret's text yesterday. It's a magical place to be when you've got a lot of things to get done, but it can sometimes elude us when we need it the most.

So how do you get into this wonderful state of flow? It's not magic that creates it. A combination of things add up to you being able to focus deeply on what you're doing. If you want to tap into that more often, you can take steps to help trigger it.

Have somewhere to work that has no physical distractions. If you're lucky enough to have complete control over where you work, choose somewhere quiet with no other people. Limit physical objects in your workspace to only the things you need for your work.

Take care of any quick, urgent tasks before you sit down to a big task that needs focus. If it's going to take less than ten minutes to clear an urgent task off the list, then do that task asap. You'll concentrate better without that task at the back of your mind.

To achieve a real state of 'flow' you do need to be skilled at the task. So if it's a new skill, your focus should be on becoming more confident in it, so that you can eventually hit that 'flow' state.

Researchers have also linked general happiness with being in a state of flow. It's not completely clear exactly why the two are linked. However, higher productivity, a sense of achievement and the ability to tune out all other thoughts and worries while you work are bound to improve your mood!

Deep Work vs. Shallow Work
Not all work is going to need, or will even allow you to enter a state of flow. When you look at your to-do list, there will be tasks on the list that are short or don't require much skill. These aren't tasks that will allow you to get into a true flow state.

For example, making a phone call to pay a bill isn't going to induce, or require, a state of flow, it's shallow work. Writing an essay, analyzing data, painting a picture, however, are all deep work tasks that benefit from a state of flow.

Shallow work is still necessary work. They're the tasks that keep the day-to-day moving smoothly and make the deep work possible. Deep work is most likely to be the tasks that are moving you closer to your goals.

Deep work isn't just the kind of work that requires you to sit at a desk, however. A photographer taking nature shots, a footballer playing a crucial game, an engineer fixing complex machinery. These are all examples of deep work beyond the kind spent sat at a computer. They all still require the person doing them to be in the moment and completely and utterly focused on the task before them.

The point is that it's the deep work that moves you forward, and it needs deep focus to get it done.

The Key To Eliminating Distractions

Distractions are the enemy of focus. To reach a state of

flow, you're going to need to remove, or at the very least minimize all distractions.

It takes roughly ten minutes from beginning a task for you to be completely focused on it. After this, the average person can sustain concentration for roughly 20 more minutes before needing a break. If you do get interrupted during your state of flow, some studies show that it can take up to 15 minutes to regain your focus. So, eliminating distractions is well worth it to keep your state of flow.

If you can carve out 30-40-minute blocks of uninterrupted time, you can drastically increase your productivity. Even better, with sustained practice, you can reach deep focus faster, and maintain it for longer. It's easier said than done, however. We've discussed a few times now how turning off your phone and switching off email notifications can help you get more productive. If you're not doing it already, then it's time to implement it.
Let's tackle the most probably ways we distract ourselves first:

Social Media and the Internet.
Turn off your cell phone and switch off Wi-Fi to reduce the risk of you checking social media or becoming distracted by a notification. Resist the urge to fact-check or research on the internet and try to keep research and note-taking as a separate task. If possible, just make a note of what you need to check and then move on. Do the actual checking later.

Our own thoughts.
Keep a notepad and pen handy. When a distracting thought pops into your head, just write it down. That way, you can ignore it and not have it nagging at you while you try to focus.

Taking erratic breaks.
Schedule regular breaks of 5-15 minutes per hour. You can use them to get a drink of water, have a snack, take a quick walk, do any printing or photocopying. Doing something that means you must get up from your desk helps to keep you active and gives your body a stretch after a long period sitting down. Try not to use these breaks to check emails as then it's very easy to get sucked into something else. Instead, carve out a couple of blocks of time each day where you deal with only emails.

Next let's deal interruptions from others:

Protect your time.
Schedule time for deep work and make sure everybody knows you are not to be disturbed. If you use your planner to schedule times where you are available, people won't feel like you're trying to shut them out. If there are times of the day that you know you get a lot of interruptions, keep those as free as possible. You can use these times to tackle any small, quick shallow focus tasks.

Turn off your cell phone.
We covered this repeatedly already, but it makes a huge difference. It's not just the temptation to check social media that's an issue. Another reason to turn it off is so that people can't get in touch and distract you. The sound of your phone ringing will definitely pull you out of a flow state.

Work somewhere that nobody can find you.
Unfortunately, many of us have little choice in where we work from. Open-plan offices are the norm, and if you happen to have been allocated the desk by the entrance then

you're going to have people walking past you all day. If you're by the water cooler, you'll not only get foot traffic but possibly the opportunity to eavesdrop on all the office gossip. It might be interesting, but it's not helpful for your focus. If you have to work in a noisy area, and you can't move, then consider using white noise apps or soundtracks; or listening to classical music to help you focus better and tune out those distractions.

Schedule.
If possible, start early, or schedule work for times that the people who tend to distract you are not available. You've probably noticed how getting to the office early can often mean you get more done in an hour or two than you would otherwise during an entire day!

The Pomodoro Method

So, now we know that you can train yourself to reach deep focus more easily and to concentrate for longer periods of time. But how, exactly, do you implement this? Even after you successfully eliminate distractions, it can still be difficult to sit down and get the work done. This is where the Pomodoro Method comes in.

Created by Francesco Cirillo in the late 1980s, The Pomodoro Method is an amazingly simple, brilliantly effective way to build a focus habit. Cirillo named the technique after a tomato-shaped kitchen timer used to implement the technique.

All you need to get started is a timer. You can use a kitchen timer (tomato shape not required!), a stopwatch, internet pages or your phone's alarm function or timer. You can even download an app for your smartphone that will track your intervals for you.

Almost everyone has access to a timer of some kind so there are no excuses not to give this a try. You can use it next time you have a task scheduled that needs deep focus and that you have planned into your schedule. It can be any size task you like as long as it's something you want to get done.

Step One: Set your timer for 25 minutes. By setting the timer, you are committing to giving this task 100% of your focus for the next 25 minutes. You won't be checking your phone, your emails, or doing any other task at all for the next 25 minutes.

Step Two: When the timer starts, you start working, and you **Do. Not. Stop** until those 25 minutes are up. If an unexpected interruption happens, postpone or ignore it unless it's a real and genuine emergency.

Step Three: When the timer goes off, stop working on the task. Make a quick note of what you managed to achieve in your 25 minutes.

Step Four: Set the timer for 5 minute. Take a short break to grab a drink, use the bathroom and stretch your legs.

Now, start again and repeat steps 1-4. When you've completed 4 Pomodoro sets of 25 minutes, take a 30-minute break.

If you can't carve out a couple of hours of time to work solidly, then you can just do 2 Pomodoro sets. Wherever possible though, make the time to do a full 4 sets. A lot of people do 4 in the morning and 4 in the afternoon, and those 4-5 hours are the most productive in their day.

Improve your Deep Focus with Pomodoro

You can use Pomodoro to train the length of your focus time. Once the 25minute timer seems to be too short, you can extend by 5 minutes each time, until you reach 40-50minute sessions with 10minute breaks. Don't go over 50 minutes as you do need regular breaks to maintain focus. If you put the timer up and find it hard to maintain focus for that amount of time, just reduce it again. It's important that you get the most out of each Pomodoro segment. If making them longer isn't achieving that goal then there's no reason to increase them.

You'll probably find that you get a lot more done in 25 minutes than you thought was possible. When you commit to complete focus and sustain it, you create a habit of getting into the 'flow.' Over time, you will come to associate your timer of choice with the habit of getting in the flow, and it will become almost effortless.

Pomodoro works well for almost everybody. Impatient people like it because anyone can focus for 25 minutes, and that's all you need to commit to for each segment. People who like structure enjoy it because it's a methodical yet simple way of working that is easy to measure. People who don't like structure like it because it's not too prescriptive. You choose the task you work on, and you only commit to completing small chunks. You can even work on a different task for your next segment if you so choose, or if the previous task is completed.

Another benefit of Pomodoro is that you can begin to predict how long tasks will take. If you can outline an essay or a blog post in one segment, and write 500 words in each subsequent segment, you can predict how many segments a similar task might need.

You can also start to see when you have the most energy and how your focus is affected by times of the day. If your Pomodoro segments are more productive in the morning, then you know to concentrate them there.

Pomodoro is also a great way to make any task manageable. If you've been procrastinating, try taking the positive action of allocating some Pomodoro segments to the task gets you focused. The knowledge that it's only 25 minutes makes any task feel less daunting to tackle. You're never far from a break, so if you start to flag, it's easier to push through.

When you know that your 25 minutes is dedicated to one task, it makes it easier to stay on task and not let yourself start multi-tasking or taking unplanned breaks. Whatever that notification on your smartphone was, it can wait until your next break because it's not too far away.

Real Life Case Study: Jane

Jane is a freelance grant writer, working with various non-profits. Her goal was to increase her income and pay off her mortgage early so that she can retire in the next 10 years. To do this, she worked out that she would need to increase her income by 25%.

Jane gets paid per completed grant application, and so to increase her income, she would need to be able to write more grants. She already worked 4 hour weeks and didn't want to increase her working hours. When she came across the Pomodoro Method, she decided to give it a try and see if she could increase her output.

Her normal working day was made up of four hours in the morning, and four in the afternoon. Alongside the actual grant writing, she also needed to make time for client calls, research, and marketing efforts. She decided to incorporate four Pomodoro segments in the morning, a break for lunch, and then to tackle the other work in the afternoon.

Her output was usually one completed grant application per week. By her second week of using the Pomodoro technique in the mornings, she had already completed three grant applications. She was so impressed that she decided to implement another two Pomodoro sessions in the afternoon, specifically for research. Her research also sped up considerably, and she was now able to consistently complete five to six grant applications each month, instead of four. She'd even managed to exceed her goal of 25% more income.

Even more impressively, her application success rate also increased. By improving her focus and getting into a 'flow' state regularly, the quality of her work also improved allowing her to increase her rates and add even more into her retirement fund.

We're almost at the end of your time management journey. Throughout this book, we've looked at various tips and techniques to make the most of your time. In the next, and final, chapter we'll look at the different tools available to help you implement these techniques, automate simple processes and make the most of your time.

Chapter 10 – Easy and Quick Productivity Helpers

"If you want to make good use of your time, you've got to know what's most important and then give it all you've got."
Lee Iacocca

Now you have all the techniques and information that you need to begin to manage your time like a pro. Throughout this book, we've briefly mentioned some apps and tools that are available that can help you get organized and manage your time. So, in this final chapter, we'll take a closer look at these tools and how to use them to supercharge your time management efforts.

Project Management Tools

How often have you jotted down a shopping list and forgotten to take it shopping with you? Digital to-do lists are the perfect solution for most of us who have our smartphones with us when we leave the house. It's the one thing you tend to never leave without these days, right!

They make it so easy. You can capture all your tasks, check them off when they're done and track your progress. Even the most basic, free to-do list apps allow you to keep multiple lists. Some also allow prioritization.

Wunderlist is an excellent free option with lists that you can share with colleagues, friends or family members, color code and prioritize. It's also fairly easy to use.

Todoist is another good app that integrates with a couple of the other tools we'll discuss later. There's a free version that includes color coding, sub-tasks, and priorities; or a paid version with filters and push notifications. Both are user-friendly and powerful tools.

These are just a couple of the most popular apps. There are literally hundreds of to-do list smartphone apps, and the majority of them are free so you can try them until you find one that's right for you.

If you have multiple, or complex, goals and tasks to keep track of, a project management tool can help you keep on top of things. They are typically designed for working teams, but they have plenty of practical features that make them perfect for managing and monitoring progress towards individual goals.

There are lots of these tools available, and many of them have a free option. If you need more detailed tools or have a lot of projects, you can usually upgrade to extra features for a small fee. Here's a quick rundown of some of the popular options.

Trello is a very popular tool, because it integrates smoothly with other applications like **Google Drive** and **Dropbox**, and is easy to use. The free option allows you to create several boards, each with their own to-do lists, and set deadlines to help you manage your projects and tasks.

You can also choose one integration on the free plan–so you can link it to your calendar, or have it connect to Google Drive, among others. If you want to use more than one integration, there are monthly paid options to allow for that.

Trello works with boards, where you add lists made up of information cards. Each card can hold as much information as you need about the task, including any useful links, file attachments, and even a checklist to break the task down into sub-tasks. You can prioritize tasks, mark them as completed and even assign them to other people. There's also a smartphone app so that you can be organized on the go.

Asana is another, very similar option that offers an online task list and project tracker, and is free to use for the basic version. It's slightly less visual than Trello but is another great option.

Monday is yet another alternative to Trello, with many of the same features and some additional ones. It's not free, however, and is best suited to people running a business or who have multiple and complex projects.

Automation Tools

We discussed in Chapter 6 how automating some key tasks can free up your time, but we didn't go into the detail of how to do that. If you're not familiar with automation apps and tools, then get ready to have your mind blown!

One of the most popular smartphone automation apps is *IFTTT (If This, Then That)*. It's a tool that allows you to program different 'recipes' to be run when certain conditions are met. For example: If I post on Facebook, then post the same text on my Twitter account.

There are literally hundreds of pre-designed recipes, so you don't need to be a technical whizz to use these. Some examples are:

- Automatically setting your phone to silent when Google Calendar shows you as in a meeting.
- Track the hours you spend at a particular location–very useful for checking how many hours a day you spend in the office.
- Automatically create a task in ToDoist if you star a Gmail email.
- Post your Facebook and Instagram photos to Twitter–saving you time re-posting it yourself.

There are so many more available that you'd be hard pressed not to find some useful ones. Depending on what other apps and tools you use, you could be automating hundreds of little tasks!

Another one is **Zapier,** which integrates with a lot of other apps and software via what they call 'zaps.' It's not completely free, depending on how many 'zaps' you want to use. The actual processes you can automate will depend on what you currently use. Some great things you can do with Zapier include:
1) Create a Trello card when you attach a specific label to a Gmail email.
2) Get a daily email alert for Instagram hashtag mentions–saving you checking Instagram.
3) Automatically save email attachments to Google Drive, Dropbox or OneDrive
4) Automate your file management processes and auto-save to your cloud storage.

Tools like this can pick up multiple small tasks. Not only do you save the minutes it would have taken you to complete the task, but you're also avoiding multitasking and context switching! Plus, things like file management automation means you'll never lose valuable time looking for an important file again.

Tracking Apps

If you spend a lot of time on your computer, and you want to avoid falling down the internet distraction rabbit hole, there are tools to help you track your online activity. Some of these will even calculate your productive time for you and track this over days, weeks, and months.

They're great for collecting data in the background that you can review monthly to see where you can take back some time. Just don't let yourself fall into the trap of spending time daily looking at your data, it's a time drain in itself.

Rescue Time is a very popular option, with a Lite version, and a premium version. With the Lite option, you can track the time you spend on websites and your desktop apps to calculate how productive you are.

You can also get a report via email each week that breaks down where you spent your time. You can set goals for a productive time and have access to 3 months' worth of data. The premium version has additional features such as blocking certain sites that you know can be a time drain, and access to all historical data.

Toggl is another option for tracking your time, and the free version has lots of features including a Pomodoro Timer. Where Rescue Time will automatically track your computer usage, Toggl requires you to start tracking manually, by pushing the timer button.

You can track the time you spend on different projects and add labels to projects so you can report on how much time you spend on each goal or project. The only downside is if you forget to track your work by starting the timer–or forget to stop the timer!

Toggl has a mobile app too, so you can track what you're doing from anywhere.

Internet Blocking Apps
You can get versions of these for your desktop and for your smart devices. They will shut off all internet access on your device, and non-essential apps from your phone, for a pre-determined amount of time.

You will still be able to make and receive phone calls and text messages in case of an emergency. Most other apps like Facebook, Twitter, and Candy Crush will all be on lockdown until the timer runs out.
It's a pretty effective method for those of us who overuse our smartphones and find ourselves losing time checking notifications.

There are lots of these available, but the one you choose will depend on the type of work you need to get done. As the world moves more and more towards cloud-based working, people need the flexibility to block only certain kinds of activities. It's not always necessary to block the entire internet (which could be easily achieved by turning off your WiFi!).

For example, **Freedom** can either block all internet access on your desktop or only selected sites. You can choose to block all social media, for example, but still be able to access work-related websites.

Freedom isn't actually free, but they do have a free trial so that you can see if it works for you.
If you're a **Google Chrome** user, the browser extension

Stay Focused allows you to set an acceptable time limit for websites and blocks them once you go over it. You can set up blocked lists and allowed lists to give you control over what you can and can't access. The pop-up warnings if you set yourself very lenient time allowances are also fairly amusing!

For a free service, it's fairly comprehensive other than it will only work with Google Chrome. There's even a 'nuclear' option that can't be switched off. If you're a **Firefox** user, **LeechBlock** will do a similar job.

On your smartphone, **Flipd** is a great option for blocking access to non-essential apps for the time you set. If you want something a little less drastic, **Moment** on IOS and Appblock on Android devices are great choices that allow you to customize which apps you want to restrict access to.

Audiobooks
If one of your goals is to read more, then consider incorporating audiobooks into your life. They're perfect for while you're ironing and doing chores, commuting or jogging, etc. They're an ideal example of one of the few times when multitasking can work, provided they're used while you're doing an 'autopilot' kind of task. Remember the type I described in the chapter on deep focus? They're also great for relaxing in the evening when you want to unwind.

Most of the native music players in your smartphone will play audiobooks, but the most popular audiobook app is *Audible*. It allows you to change the speed of the narration so that you can 'read' the book faster. You can also listen to audiobooks via the app you didn't purchase from Audible if you prefer, thus saving time by having them all in one place.

A Word of Warning
Tools are great but don't go overboard using the tools. It's easy to spend a lot of time looking at the tools to assess your progress, and that's time better spent working towards your goals. Don't let them become a new procrastination technique where you spend hours unnecessarily organizing your Trello boards or analyzing your Rescue Time data.

By all means use the tools discussed here, just be mindful of the fact that they should be helping and not hindering your time management.

Real Life Case Study: Linda

Linda is a busy working mom and hair salon owner. She needed all the help she could get in organizing her life and her work. After investigating the options available to her, she successfully used a combination of tools to streamline and organize her both her work and home life.

She created Trello Boards for her key life goals, allowing her to see her to-do list and track progress towards goals. She created a board for salon tasks like ordering supplies and created another for repetitive housekeeping tasks, some of which she delegated out to family members via Trello.

As a busy salon owner, she was finding that keeping up with her various social media channels was a big drain on her time. Beyond the time it took to post on the various channels, when she logged in, she would often get distracted scrolling the feeds and lose time she could have been working.

She created IFTTT scripts to post automatically to social media any photographs that she saved to the album 'hair transformations.' This allowed her to keep her business social media active, filled with before and after photos of clients, without her needing to even log in.

For her back office admin, she set a Zapier zap up to automate her file management system, saving her time organizing folders and files. She also set it to save email attachments in her Dropbox file, meaning she could access these easily.

One of her personal goals was to renovate the kitchen by herself. At home in the evenings, she used Flipd to prevent her becoming distracted by her phone and set to work on the tasks as broken down on her Trello board. She had set a 6 month timeline to have the DIY project completed, but managed it in 4 months, thanks to her new-found organization and time management.

Get More Done In Life. Keep Calm. Be In Control.

So, now you know some of the most effective ways to manage your time. None of this is relevant, however, if you don't put the information to good use. If you haven't already, commit to making changes to the way you work that will help you gain back more time.

It's not a one-time project to improve your time management. It takes diligent practice to build habits that keep you efficient. Even then life has a way of changing over time so that you will need to regularly review and reassess your time management practice.

At least once a quarter you should be re-evaluating your goals and your tasks, clearing out any time clutter that has accumulated and celebrating any successfully achieved goals. Your goals may need adjusting, and that's not a failure, merely a fact of life. Events such as having children, getting married, separating from a partner or getting a new job are all common reasons that our priorities and our goals change.

It's important to be realistic. You should make an effort to implement the tips and techniques outlined in this book; simply reading it won't magically create more time for you. However, not every day will go to plan, and sometimes you will fail. Don't beat yourself up about it. The key is to create long-standing habits. If you miss something one day simply pick back up again the next day – or as soon as you are able.

Here's a quick recap of some of the key points we've covered:

- You must set goals and understand your 'why.' If you're

not aiming for something specific, you'll never get there. Write your goals down and review them regularly.

- Multi-tasking actually harms your productivity. Instead, try to focus on one task at a time to get the benefits of being in a flow state.

- Eliminate distractions as much as you can, and avoid allowing social media and other unproductive activities to sneak into your work time.

- Self-care is essential. Get enough sleep, drink lots of water and eat healthy foods, get some exercise, make time for meditation. Your mind and body will thank you for it, and you'll become more productive in the long run when you're less tired and stressed.

- There's almost always a root cause of procrastination, often related to either fear or motivation. Find the root cause, and you can often eliminate your procrastination habit.

The benefits you can expect to see from following the tips and techniques in this book consistently are:
- Improved productivity without working harder or longer hours.
- Less stress and more time for self-care.
- More clarity around your goals and renewed focus on achieving your goals.
- A better understanding of how you are using your time.

When you're evaluating your time management, be honest with yourself, but also be kind too. This is a way of life and not a quick-fix boot camp. If you're falling short in some areas, you can simply take some positive action to fix that. Don't worry about yesterday, just focus on using today to make tomorrow the best it can be.

You have enough time to achieve anything you want to. It's time to go and achieve it!

www.ingramcontent.com/pod-product-compliance
Lightning Source LLC
Chambersburg PA
CBHW031421210526
45464CB00005B/1992